FROM PRISON CELL TO MILLIONAIRE

FRANZ SZAWRONSKI

authorHOUSE®

AuthorHouse™
1663 Liberty Drive
Bloomington, IN 47403
www.authorhouse.com
Phone: 833-262-8899

Published by AuthorHouse 09/03/2020

ISBN: 978-1-7283-7346-1 (sc)
ISBN: 978-1-7283-7344-7 (hc)
ISBN: 978-1-7283-7345-4 (e)

Library of Congress Control Number: 2020917330

Print information available on the last page.

This book is printed on acid-free paper.

In the world, there are people who leave roads full of good things to follow, imitate, and improve upon, while others only leave mud to clean.

—Juan Santacoloma

ACKNOWLEDGMENTS

I want to dedicate this book to the wonderful people God has brought into my life. Of course, first off, to my mother and father for not letting me give up. In prison, I remember feeling that my life had ended completely and thinking I would have been better off dead, but then my mother came to see me, and she gave me strength. She had no idea how she helped me to believe in myself and seek God for the strength to keep going. Thanks, Mom! Dad, I thank you for your forgiveness for my being a complete dumbass and a bad kid. I'm serious! I did terrible things, and I hurt you, and still, you showed me unconditional love, forgiving me and becoming a great father to me. You are a great man.

I also want to mention my grandfather Weaver. When I was in one of the worst county jails, having to fight to keep my food, I called him on the phone, and he prayed for me and told me that was not the way for me. He said God could change anything. My grandfather died a few years ago, but I often remember his words.

I cannot forget my brother, who was very young when I left him behind and went to prison. I know that affected you, and I was not a good example to follow. I am very sorry. I love seeing the man and the incredible father you've become. I love you, my brother, and I hope you can forgive me.

Also, to my amazing sisters, Laura and Angela. I remember when we were little, we stayed up talking all night on Christmas Eve, and I used to fall asleep on the floor in your room. You two are amazing mothers and people. I thank you because although you did not understand why I did the things I did, the two of you continued to pray for me. Those prayers helped me not to give up on life. Thank you very much, Laura and Angela.

Of course, I cannot forget all my children: my son and daughter from my first marriage and my two other little angels with my current wife. I love the four of you, and I hope you become better people than I was and do not make the same mistakes I made in my life. You all encourage me every day just by my seeing or remembering your smiles and thinking of all the good qualities each of you has.

Last but not least, I want to thank my beautiful and lovely wife for entering my life and for teaching me to be honest with myself and showing me what it really is to be a father, even now that we are both learning together. I love you so much, and I am grateful to have you in my life. I really mean it when I say there is no one else like you. We have a lot of fun just being ourselves, and I have grown to love you more and more every day. Thanks for being you, my love.

Thank you all for loving me unconditionally. I hope reading this book will open the eyes of those who feel that life is over and that they have no value. I want to give hope to those who are in prison, either emotionally or physically, to realize that they can achieve anything they want to through hard work and dedication and that they should never accept what others think of them but should just believe in what God thinks of them.

As everyone knows, we are all children of God, created in his image. Please, brothers and sisters, believe and achieve the impossible.

INTRODUCTION

I think we've all heard and even used the phrase "Help yourself, and I will help you." Many people claim that God said it or that it is in the Bible, but apparently, that is false. However, there is nothing truer than that statement: "Help yourself, and I will help you." In life, there are two types of people: those who remain quiet at home or at work and remain frozen all their lives and those who take risks and go out in search of new adventures and new horizons. I am a man who has had to pass through many dark and difficult roads. Since I was a child at home, deficiencies and problems were part of the daily menu from breakfast to lunch, and even that was just what we had to eat.

I was born in an area where young people saw gangsters as big shots with nice cars, lots of money, luxuries, vices, and women. From the street corners, we watched them, like when a cat stalks a mouse but doesn't dare to make the final leap. That was how my friends and I were. We spent a lot of time admiring these characters we considered almost otherworldly. We wanted to be like them—yes, like criminals. They were the mirrors that we, disadvantaged kids, used to look into to see our futures reflected. Nothing could have been more absurd and incoherent. But that was life back then in my little neighborhood where I grew up. It was a place of Italian mobsters, and their word was the law.

It was not easy to grow up there under those circumstances. All the young people sooner or later were involved in some way in that criminal underworld. Of course, I was no exception; I also participated in those almost Machiavellian maneuvers to disarm justice and act on our own whims and convenience, but always, in everything and at all times, we were watched and supervised by the great bosses of that powerful Mafia.

I have many stories and anecdotes from my boyhood years, but I have many other better ones lived after leaving that dark and obscure environment to which one had to succumb and which impregnated me in the most remote and hidden fibers of myself. That world is difficult to enter, but once you are inside, it is much more difficult to leave, especially alive.

For negative and adverse reasons, I was presented with the opportunity to change my life in a radical way. I spent many sleepless nights thinking over what to do with my life and my future. I did not have the slightest idea what I was going to do. I only knew how to do what I had learned in my neighborhood with my friends.

I used to love sports, and I was good at soccer, but that was not something that convinced me enough to devote myself fully and completely to being a dedicated player. I went back again and again to the same question of what to do, and I just didn't know. I did not have even a remote understanding of what was going to happen with my life or what I wanted my life to be like.

The important thing is to believe in ourselves and our own capabilities. Human beings, with all their greatness, have indescribable qualities unknown even to themselves waiting to be touched upon and stimulated to emerge with all their enormity and to demonstrate everything of which they are capable.

Success is a subjective term and depends largely on the needs, desires, ambitions, and aspirations of each person. There are other factors, such as education, the environment in which one lives, and the socioeconomic stratum, that can affect to a greater or lesser extent the nature of what success means to a person. We must keep in mind that success is personal, and what one person sees as success another might not.

Each person has, according to his or her own personality, plans, and style, things he or she wants to achieve. For some, these are small and simple things, but for others, they are large and complicated. Achieving them depends on people's decision and commitment to themselves and to the goals they set for themselves.

We should never criticize the goals and objectives of others. Each goal is personal and is as important and valid as our own. In the world, there will be people who think your goals and objectives are small and insignificant. That being said, it is important to give value to all people for who they are, what they represent, what they want to be, and what they want to achieve. We should not minimize or disregard the scope of their success. Each person's objectives, just like your own, are the most important to him or her. They are the reason for living. They are the reason to work hard; put forth all your effort and desire; make huge sacrifices; and, in short, dedicate your life to your own cause.

In talking about dedicating your life to your own cause in what you are looking for and what you want, I want to give you an example of the difference between being committed and being simply involved.

I think many of us have enjoyed an excellent and delicious plate of ham and eggs, so let's analyze the ham and eggs to see what it means to be involved and be committed. In this example, there are two animals that participate: the chicken to lay the egg and the pig to provide the ham.

The chicken only lays its egg—that's it. Its participation is minimal because there is nothing unique about laying an egg; nothing out of the ordinary is involved. We are all happy to have chickens that give us their eggs to consume every day around the world.

On the other hand, in order to obtain the ham, it is necessary that the poor pig loses its life. The pig must be totally committed for us to enjoy our ham and eggs. Life seems cruel, but both animals fulfill their roles.

This is exactly what I mean. When you decide to embark on a new adventure or your first adventure, it's important that you keep these two concepts in mind: get involved, and get committed.

If you really want and intend to succeed, you have to stop being an observer. Participate, get involved, commit, and do everything to achieve what you really want. You have to leave your shell, your comfort zone, to achieve personal success. No matter what happens, no matter how big or small a project is, each personal project is always huge and deserves all of our attention and dedication. If it is our first project, it is much more important to dedicate all our strengths and get fully involved on a personal level to be successful. Success will depend on you and your commitment.

Are you willing to dedicate enough and leave it all on the field so your success becomes a beautiful reality? Or do you prefer to remain mediocre and without ambitions?

If you are the first kind of person I mentioned, I suggest you continue reading so you can learn and expand your motivation. If you are the second kind of person, stop here, close the book, and ask for your money back because this book is not for you. Don't waste your time.

To be a successful person, you have to achieve many goals, work hard, and never falter.

I am reminded of a poem I read in school that represents a little of what I want to express and share with all of you in this book. The author is John Greenleaf Whittier (1807–1892). His poem is titled "Don't Quit":

When things go wrong as they sometimes will,
When the road you're drudging seems all uphill,
When the funds are low, and the debts are high,
and you want to smile but you have to sigh.
When care is pressing you down a bit.
Rest if you must but don't you quit!
Life is queer with its twists and turns,
as everyone of us sometimes learns.
And many a failure turns about
When he might have won had he stuck it out.
Don't give up though the pace seems slow—
you may succeed with another blow.
Success is failure turned inside out—
the silver tint of the cloud of doubt.
And you never can tell how close you are.
It may be near when it seems so far.
So stick to the fight when you're hardest hit—
it's when things seem worst that you must not quit.

I don't think I need to explain much about the meaning of those beautiful words. Just keep going with your ideas and your dreams. Don't abandon them! They will feed you, and they will nourish your soul, your spirit, and your being. Please do not give up!

When I was a kid, my family didn't go to restaurants or even eat hamburgers. We watched the other kids eat their hamburgers, while we had to settle for the delicious food Mom used to prepare. It was always the same, and it didn't look as appetizing as a fresh, juicy, huge hamburger with tomato, onion, and lettuce on a soft and rich bun that seemed as if it would split while you ate it. Oh, and not to mention the bubbly, cold soda next to the plate, which showed the exquisiteness of the hamburger. That was my childhood, and the truth is, it didn't change much during those early years.

Every day, life gives us its wonders and lessons, and although for many, the dawn is a pain due to illness, poverty, misery, or just laziness, it is always extraordinary to have the opportunity to live another day and have the chance to breathe, share, feel, run, laugh, cry, create, produce, and do hundreds of other things. Maybe that's what has helped me to get where I am today: I always go out in search of something. I don't wait for things to come to me—quite the contrary. I face each situation with integrity and acceptance so that it doesn't bend me, no matter how strong it seems.

Obviously, I've had moments of weakness and times when I thought that I was going to pale or break or that taking a rest could help. But no, definitely not. Those times used to rest can be counterproductive and distracting, especially if we are working or fighting for some cause or reason.

You must never leave things halfway done once you start them. You always have to finish before taking a break, especially if what you face represents a problem or difficulty that requires all of your attention. Just as a break could be convenient for you, likewise, it could be convenient for the people or situations that stand in your way, those that in some way represent your problem or difficulty.

You should accomplish each task before thinking about taking a break or vacation. This has been part of my philosophy of life, and believe me, it has given me a lot of results, maybe even since I was a child, when I saw and lived situations that not many children have to deal with throughout their lives.

1

MEMORIES OF MY EARLY YEARS

My father was always a brave and hardworking man determined to accomplish many things. He did, but different situations ended up undermining our relationship, and unfortunately, he did not share much time with the family. Of course, because his behavior he worked out his future and the lifestyle he leads today. He always had a blessing, since he married my mother. She stood firm next to him, her husband, the one she swore to love and respect all her life, and she still does to this day.

My father arrived in the United States when he was only nine years old. His story is full of impressive anecdotes, especially those about his life as a child and the difficulties his family faced as a result of the Second World War.

He was a working man, always looking for money to pay the bills at home, and I must confess, I suspect he paid the bills in some other places as well, because we struggled to survive.

He landed in New York, and from there, he made his own way in this country. He started working when he was very young, and he worked as many jobs as he could. He played football, and he received a scholarship, but he had to become responsible to start supporting a family that was in the way. He worked in the scrap metal business and in car sales, and he had his own restaurant. He carried out a great variety of jobs in order to be ready for the arrival of his first daughters, who were twins.

I don't remember much of him in those years, only that he had a difficult life and was very strict. He used to work a lot, and he was not a violent person. Sometimes several days and nights passed when I did not even see him. Of course, my mother was worried about those long absences, which he justified with his job and the necessity to support our family.

As a young guy, I had several differences with my dad, and I had to act as the man of the house in many instances while my mom was sick. My two sisters had some differences with my dad as well.

Sometimes, at my mother's request, we used to go out at night looking for him. We were young and maybe did not understand the reality. My mother used to tell us we were going to eat doughnuts or something so she could go see where he was and what he was doing. Later, I understood that whom he was with was also important to my mother.

I started to feel a deep hatred for my father, a person I didn't see but whom I had to call Dad. I kept those and other feelings for a long time. Of course, that was the perception of a little kid who didn't understand the reality of the situation and who was not aware of the whole context of that reality that he saw and lived from his standpoint.

Now my father is elderly, but he still works and is with my mother, who loyally accompanies him and helps him on his journeys. They manage their own real estate business. They fix up the houses by themselves to put them on the market. It seems to be a good business.

My poor mother, Nancy, a descendant of Italians who arrived in the United States, has suffered a great deal with this situation, and over the years, these sufferings and sorrows took their toll.

My mother is a wonderful woman who always cared for and watched over her children. She was always humble and tremendously honest. She never lied and did not like to be lied to. She cared for us as long as she could, always protecting us and watching over our well-being.

She was born with beautiful brown eyes that were a perfect match for her light skin. She is thin and five feet two inches tall. Loving and always caring, she took care of us and gave us the best of herself. Today she is still that tender woman, and at her advanced age, she deserves only the best and most sacred things in the world.

Although my mother was not very affectionate, she always made us feel her love. To the best of her ability, she maintained a relationship with each one of her children. She is reassuring like no other, which is one of the qualities I admire most about her, along with her honesty.

Thanks to my parents, I had the chance to meet Laura and Angela, my two older twin sisters, and my brother.

The first three women in my life were my wonderful mother, Nancy, and my sisters, Laura and Angela. All three of them have always been a vital part of every moment of my existence.

I had a wonderful relationship with my two sisters. We used to play together; we used to go to the same school; and we shared the chores at home, such as washing the dishes, cleaning, and doing other things our mom asked us to do—and Mom was very adamant.

I had such a great relationship with my sisters that from time to time, I used to sleep in their bedroom. They were around sixteen, and I was twelve or thirteen years old.

Laura, who now is a nurse, was always special and affectionate toward me. Her beautiful hair looked like gold treats that flowed gracefully as she walked or jumped. Angela, tender and beautiful since she was a little girl, used to fascinate people with her golden hair that seemed to shine with the rays of the sun.

Both of them love sports, and they always showed me what was best and were a great example to follow in my childhood. Unfortunately, I decided to follow a different path.

Angela is a special education teacher, and she is an extraordinary example to all those children who need love, experience, and professionalism. Even though she is not currently working due to homeschooling her own children, she will certainly return soon to the children who sorely need her experience and knowledge.

Nowadays, both my sisters are married, and thanks to God, they help the community in different ways with their professions, educating, helping to develop and saving lives, and easing the bodily pain of the people who surround them and need them. My sisters are two beautiful blessings in my life.

I did not have a great relationship with my younger brother or even the opportunity for one. He is four years younger than I, and maybe that, along with the life I started living as we grew up, stood in the way of our relationship.

My brother is a gentle, polite, and kind man. Like all of us, he is also engaged in sports. He is a dedicated professional in heavy machinery mechanics at a great company and loves soccer like I do. He works hard to provide for his family and cares for his two little girls.

I wouldn't say my childhood was normal. There were many things that left scars in my life and the lives of others who were close to me. People, situations, and other things both internal, at home with my family, and external, such as from the street, school, the neighborhood, and friends, exerted a great influence on my childhood.

The time and place in which I grew up turned me into a child few wanted around and for whom few, if anyone, gave a damn, including myself, because I believed I was not going to make it until eighteen years old. With the way I grew up, I was convinced I would die before I turned eighteen.

2

TIME TO GET OUT

It was a hot summer morning in August 1974. My mother was in terrible pain but still trying to prepare breakfast for my father. Apparently, he didn't realize, or just didn't care, that this woman was complaining about her pains while preparing his breakfast. My father drank his last bit of coffee and left the house as if everything were normal. My aching mother was writhing on a chair. My older sister Laura approached her and asked if she could help her in some way, but my mother could hardly speak. My sister went to get the neighbor to come see our mother. I couldn't do anything to help.

The neighbor lady arrived. She was approximately fifty years old and more than two hundred pounds. She was forever hanging around my house and the neighborhood searching for gossip and a way to use her forked tongue. She took over the house as if it were her own. She made some sort of herbal tea for my mother, told her to calm down, and said they would go to the hospital shortly. We never knew where she was from, but she had a funny accent that made her cut her words short.

The lady grabbed the phone and called the emergency number. After a few minutes, sirens and lights woke up everyone in the neighborhood. EMTs took my mother to the hospital. Upon her arrival, a group of nurses and doctors treated her almost immediately. A few hours later, one of the doctors came out and told my father, whom they had called to come to the hospital, "Congratulations! It's a boy!"

My father jumped in excitement. After two daughters, the little boy he'd wanted and longed for had arrived. That was more or less the story of my birth. My father was attentive to my mother and me, and he didn't leave us alone for a single minute.

My sisters were excited; it seemed as if I were a baby doll brought by Santa Claus on Christmas. They took care of me, carried me, soothed me, and pampered me as if I were the most precious of their toys. Of course, they both knew I was their brother and knew what I would represent in the house. Unfortunately, the lives of my two sisters had not been very fulfilling in their young ages.

My sister Laura, the older of the twins, on the many occasions when my mother was not feeling well or when my parents had a fight, took care of my other sister Angela. They comforted each other to avoid being part of the arguments my parents had.

3

ONE OF THE SCARIEST MOMENTS

That morning seemed perfect. I got up early, as I did every day, but this time, I felt a special energy. Something inside me told me it was going to be a great day. I got up and immediately put on my workout clothes and left the house with the moon lighting the way. I did some warm-up exercises before running the streets for almost an hour. My body was cold, which was why I decided to do some warm-up exercises beforehand, so as not to affect my muscles. Ten minutes after the warm-up, I started jogging while hearing car horns in the distance as cars got onto the highway.

As I crossed the streets, my speed increased, and my breathing became more rapid. I ran for almost forty-five minutes, until my body told me, "Enough! Don't abuse me anymore." I started to slow my pace, and without realizing it, I was walking home.

Everyone was already awake and getting ready for his or her daily tasks, such as school, cleaning, cooking, sports, homework, and more. My father had not come home to sleep, something that had become more common. It caused a lot of pain and sleepless nights for my poor mother. Many times, I witnessed my mom not close her eyes at all during the whole night, and that night was one of many she'd spent crying and complaining about her life and her destiny.

I showered and grabbed a snack. We didn't have much to choose from. Then I left for school after saying goodbye to my mother with a kiss on her cheek, maybe to comfort her for all the suffering that was taking a toll on her and gnawing at her or maybe just to let her know not to worry and to let my father live his life and to start living her own. But I knew she couldn't stop worrying about my father and his well-being.

On my way to school, I met some friends who always waited for me next to the park to play a little before our first class. On that particular day, I would have preferred not to go to class. It was math, and I hated it—not the subject itself but the teacher. He used to look at me as if I owed him something or as if I were an alien.

When we got to the classroom, we found out the teacher was sick and taking the day off, and a substitute teacher would be with us. Two minutes before the class started, a spectacular blonde entered the room. She had beautiful blue eyes that merged with the sky that day. I was petrified, motionless, and didn't blink. My friend pushed me to wake me up. "Wake up, silly!" he told me. That class made me realize that math and numbers would be my passion.

At that moment, I would have done anything to avoid the bell ring announcing that the class was over. I would have given anything to stay in that classroom with that teacher for a lifetime, but the bell rang, and I came back to reality. She said goodbye with a perfect smile, and I followed her with my eyes until she disappeared into the crowd.

Classes went on, and there she was in my mind, dancing among chemistry formulas, historical dates, and world capitals, until a punch in my chest woke me up. It was my friend Kenny's fist. With a soccer ball in his other hand, he told me it was time to go to practice.

That soccer ball was the one to blame for making me forget the woman who, up to that moment, was the woman of my life.

We started playing, and like always, we chose teams and practiced for a good amount of time. Soccer was something I was passionate about. I enjoyed it, and I was good at it. My friends, my coaches, and I thought I had great potential as a youth soccer player. That was the reason I used to play it with my heart, with passion and pride. Also, being a recognized athlete made me famous among the schoolgirls and made me the envy of the rest of the guys.

My friends and I playing soccer

After practice, we went to the locker room. My friends and I planned to go to the movies that night and invite some girls. That day was perfect. When I got out of the locker room, I ran into Charlynn, a beautiful brunette I'd been crazy about for weeks but had been unable to talk to, because she was always with her friends. I told myself, *This is my opportunity.* Without hesitation, I asked her out that night. After a brief silence, she said yes. I couldn't have asked for more from life that day.

On my way home, I was excited, thinking about the clothes I was going to wear to impress Charlynn. I then remembered I had to go by the store to buy milk and eggs, as my mom had asked me to do that morning. Without hesitation, I changed my direction a bit and went to the store. I was happy and confident that God had tailored that day for me.

When I arrived home, I found the door open, something that was not normal at my house. We always kept the door closed because my neighborhood wasn't the safest place in the city, and there were always people trying to take things from inside the houses. It was silent except for the sound of a person sobbing. *My mother*, I thought, *again crying because my father didn't come, didn't give her any money, or didn't tell her something.* When I went upstairs, I found out it was not my mother sobbing; it was my younger brother, almost in shock. Next to him, my mother lay as if dead in the middle of a pool of blood in the bathtub.

My brother was frozen and static, and even though I tried to make him react, he didn't. I confirmed that he was breathing by putting my hand on his chest. I then went to check on my mother. *She's dead*, I thought. She was cold to the touch. *Yeah, she is dead*, I thought again. However, when I got my ear closer to her mouth and nose, I noticed a weak breath. I tried to give her mouth-to-mouth CPR and call the emergency number at the same time, but I couldn't do both things at once.

All of a sudden, my little brother started to react, and thanks to his help, we were able to call the emergency number and ask for help.

Minutes later, my house was full of paramedics as sirens and lights swarmed the whole neighborhood. Our mother was intubated, and an artificial respirator was needed. After that, they placed her on a stretcher and got her into an ambulance to take her to the nearest hospital.

My sisters came home right in the middle of all of this happening.

Laura and I went to the hospital with our mother, while Angela stayed home to take care of our little brother.

After several tests, blood work, medications, and examinations by several specialists, the verdict was something we had never imagined. A doctor in his forties came out and walked to us, asking for Mrs. Nancy's relatives. Laura and I answered at the same time, "Yes! We're her children."

The doctor asked if an adult was with us, and Laura said, "No, we don't know where our father is, and we have no way to communicate with him."

The doctor stroked his hair and then passed his hand by her chin. "Okay," he said, "if there is no adult here to talk to and you are the only relatives around, I have to tell you that your mother's situation is serious—very serious. As you probably expect, your mother's health situation is really delicate. She is in a serious condition." Our mom had not followed the directions on her prescription medication, which was extremely dangerous.

The doctor added, "It's still too early to tell what effects and reactions these medications might cause. It's necessary that your mom stay hospitalized for a couple of days until all the medications are completely eliminated from her body, and then we'll decide what course of action to take, depending on the results of the final tests. Also, it's very important to determine how to keep the same thing from happening again."

It was imperative that our mom get additional professional care, or maybe she needed someone who stayed with her at home, the doctor said. From then on, we, her children, had to ensure our mother felt happy, comforted, calm, and free from any worries, either marital or financial.

My sister Laura and I said, "Yes, sir. Yes, sir," but deep inside, we knew that was impossible unless my father committed to make a change. But knowing him and the way he was, we knew beforehand that would be a lost cause and that our mother was going to have to overcome this situation and move forward alone. She would have our support, but the truth was, there was little we could do for her.

We were still in the hospital at almost eleven o'clock at night; many hours had passed since we had arrived. We were hungry. Our stomachs were growling, protesting for something to eat. We left the hospital. We were cold and had no money. We left our mother on the bed, in a deep sleep with no sign of coming back out of it.

While walking on the street, we got to a corner where a big poster of a movie was displayed, and I suddenly remembered my date. "Fuck! Charlynn!"

My extraordinary day, the one that had seemed to be the best, had ended in tragedy. The worst thing was that I didn't know how to explain to Charlynn what had happened. Indeed, I did not even know if I would have the chance to talk to her again.

4

THE LITTLE ONE IN THE HOUSE

In spite of the fact that my relationship with my father was not the best, that he was practically never home because he was always working, and that he was the cause for all the trouble and wrongs with my mother, I must recognize that he was and is a working man.

Since his arrival in the United States, he hasn't stopped working. If money earned was based on time and effort, without a doubt, my father would be a millionaire because he has dedicated each minute of his adult life to work. I know of many different jobs he performed during my childhood.

Just like his father, my grandfather, who was a carpenter, he started doing that job as a legacy. However, he worked many different jobs, from mechanic to carpenter to car salesman. He worked in restaurants and in the real estate business, buying houses to fix them up and then put them on the market. Just imagine a job, and picture my father doing it. No matter what his profession was, he excelled at it.

I remember one job in particular that influenced my life. You soon will know why.

At home, we always were in need, and I was a witness to the needs and sufferings of my mother and my sisters and the almost daily deficiencies with which we lived during my childhood. I had to work to somehow, and with little, be able to help my mother with the expenses that were constantly pressuring us.

I tried to find something to do during the summer and on the weekends to make some money. My father's new job was the perfect opportunity for this.

I went to talk to my father and told him I wanted to work. Since my father started working very young, he didn't see anything abnormal in that situation. He didn't hesitate and accepted. In addition, I think it was an advantage for him because he knew in advance that the little money I earned was going to end up in the hands of my mother. Therefore, it was money he was going to save, as there was going to be a little more money in the house without it necessarily coming out of his pocket. He told me that the job was not going to be easy and that I would have to follow the rules and work like every other one of his employees. He wouldn't allow me to start trouble or encourage others not to meet his expectations because I was his son.

He told me about my job, gave me a short tour of the facilities, and quickly explained the restaurant management process. He showed me my workplace and was clear about the importance of my job: speed, concentration, and, above all, the efficiency and effectiveness of my work mattered. Over time, I realized the normal operation of the restaurant depended to a large extent on my work. It's simple: without clean plates and utensils, you can't cook or serve food.

That first day was hard. Hundreds of plates, forks, spoons, bowls, and cups went through my hands. I had to wash, dry, and arrange them as quickly as possible. The clients would not wait, and the pace of the restaurant allowed me no time at all, not even to go to the restroom.

After three hours of continuous work, I was able to take a break and eat something. When I started washing again, it was even worse because the pots, pans, and kitchen utensils had to be washed and dried in order for the cooks to start cooking again. The rules stated that after each meal, every kitchen utensil had to be washed in order to be ready for the next shift. It took me almost two hours to wash all the utensils.

When I was almost done, one of the cooks gave me a broom and a mop and told me, "When you finish there, sweep and mop so the floor is clean and not greasy, to avoid anyone having an accident."

From a window facing the front of the restaurant, my father was looking at me with a big smile, as if saying, "You wanted to work. There you go."

But I didn't give up. I showed him that I was there to achieve big things and that no matter what work I had to do, I had a clear job. I had to work and produce, no matter what tasks they put on me. Besides, I didn't want to give my father the pleasure of seeing me defeated so easily. I had to show him that although he thought I was just a boy, I was a man, and my mother and sisters could count on me.

After a few weeks of the job, my body got used to it. I continued practicing sports, going to school, and doing my best to chip in at home.

Things were going fine, but one particular weekend, something different happened. When I arrived at the restaurant to start working, I noticed there was someone else working my shift. I was surprised and immediately went to my father to complain. When I went to face him, he was sitting next to the cashier, and it looked like he was waiting for me, because before I started talking, my father told me, "I know what you're going to say. Don't worry; you're going to keep working here, but now you are going to do another job."

Because the restaurant was doing well and the customers couldn't arrive on time, delivery was implemented, and that was to be my job. However, my father was clear with me that when we had no orders to deliver, he expected me to do something else to help—wash, sweep, or clean—because he didn't want lazy people working in the restaurant.

That was how I started delivering to the customers who couldn't or didn't want to come into the restaurant.

Sometimes, mostly afternoons, I was able to deliver up to twenty orders. My dad took the orders and gave them to the cooks to get the plates ready, and then I packaged them in their proper boxes and delivered them.

This new task was a little quieter and less draining. However, I had to deliver orders regardless of the weather, and the orders had to arrive as soon as possible, fresh and warm. That was my responsibility. I did not want anyone to call my father at the restaurant with a complaint because the food arrived cold or late. Packaging and delivering were my job.

One of the advantages of delivering was that sometimes the clients would tip, and that helped me a great deal. Every cent in my pocket was a lot of help and made a big difference to my final income.

As the days went by, I noticed that two of the cooks paid a lot of attention to my work, my speed in deliveries, and the way I performed my job at the restaurant. Not long after, the cooks talked to me and congratulated me on my job. They told me that I had a great future in interpersonal relations and that if I continued in that way, I would surely be a successful man.

Being an innocent kid, I believed their compliments about my performance and my future. Soon after, I discovered the reason for their kind words and realized where all this was going. The cooks, aware of my need and desire for money, knew in advance that I would accept other jobs I could do at same time as the deliveries without affecting my performance. The job they offered was also making deliveries. The cooks, two funny guys, contracted me to deliver the products they managed.

I was hesitant in the beginning because I knew beforehand that if my father knew about it, he would kick me and the cooks out of the restaurant. But I also wanted the extra money and felt I needed more for myself and to help at home, so without any doubt about it, I accepted their proposal, and I started making their deliveries.

I was eight years old, and I was making marijuana deliveries. Of course, back then, no one suspected an innocent child. I made many deliveries, and I can't say I didn't know what was going on. I had my doubts at the beginning, and then I confirmed them, because aside from the food deliveries, I was carrying out something else when the cooks offered me some for my own use. It didn't matter; I wasn't smoking, just delivering, and they paid me between six and eight dollars for each delivery. I used to make a couple deliveries a day.

I believe that was the first felony I committed in my life. I'd gone from an innocent child who was a dishwasher to a marijuana delivery boy. I was a small potential criminal lying dormant and waiting for someone with more experience to use him for their benefit.

Even though I knew what I was doing, I liked it. I enjoyed that whole world, and that was just the beginning of many years of even worse and more complicated problems.

5

MY MOTHER: PURE LOYALTY

My mother has always been a brave, honest, and tranquil person. She carries the truth in her hands wherever she goes, and even though she was never very affectionate, she always took care of me and my brother and sisters.

Her parents were European, but she was born in the United States. I suppose she inherited from her parents the tenacity to become the woman she is today.

The moment she met my father, they started a relationship. She was faithful, sincere, dedicated, sacrificial, and even submissive to each and every one of his demands. Despite the hard life she lived with my father, there were few times when she protested against or questioned any of his decisions. On the contrary, even when he was wrong, she supported him until the end because she wanted him to know that his woman was on his side forever.

As I said, my father was rarely home, and there were many times when his side of the bed next to my mother was cold and empty come morning. I can imagine my mom in that bed alone, dejected and sad, wondering where my father was—the man who took her to the altar, married her, and promised to be with her for life and be beside her forever. My mother suffered a lot with that situation, and I am convinced that all her health problems and bad decisions were mostly a consequence of the abandonment and desolation my father made her live in for so many years.

One time, late at night, realizing my father hadn't come home, she decided to do something different: go out to look for my father. But she couldn't leave us alone, as we were little, so she woke us up one by one and told us we were going out. "Mommy, it's late!" I told her.

"We won't be late, and on the way back, we'll stop at the doughnut store," she said.

The idea of going to get doughnuts immediately overcame my desire to stay at home, and I suppose the same happened to my siblings. With everyone in the car, my mother started driving those dark and dangerous streets.

I should have known my mother had a clear idea of where to go, though I believe she knew the area but not the exact place. We were driving around in the car for a long time—so long that we fell asleep. Suddenly, the car stopped, and she whispered to us, "I'll be back." Then she walked up to a place and went inside. Minutes later, she came out crying, and her face was red with anger.

We didn't have the slightest idea what was happening, why she went there, or what she discovered. Years later, I came to understand that late and unexpected outing. Of course, we didn't go to eat doughnuts. My mom didn't have money to pay for all of us to get doughnuts. I guess that was just a white lie from our mother.

Years went by, and our mother was always at the foot of the canyon. She recovered from all her ailments and could even abandon the medicines that filled her body with the filth that was killing her. Fortunately, perhaps as a reward for all her suffering and sacrifices but above all because of the infinite love she has for my father, today they are together, working and fighting side by side, as it always should have been.

Mother, you are a precious and wonderful example God created. I love you with all my heart!

6

MANY TROUBLES

I was not a good student. Many times, I didn't even go to school. I used to go out with my friends to do other things. I was only good at sports and playing soccer. As I said, from a young age, I used to deliver marijuana as part of my job in the restaurant. Well, that was just the beginning of a series of illegal situations I was involved in.

The neighborhood I grew up in was a quiet one but was full of drugs and mob guys, whom I admired. They always had money, women, and cars, and it seemed they had good lives and lived happily.

My friends Kenny and Jim and I thought that one day we should be in the same position as them. Unfortunately, for one of them, that idea died with him when he passed away at the age of sixteen. The news of his death caused an incredible void in us, a loneliness so great that I could not describe it, but I think the fear of being next was much greater. I was afraid the next victim would be me.

The families from my neighborhood were apparently normal, with a dad, a mom, and children who lived in a perfect relationship with the community and never missed church. They were immigrants who had settled in that area of the United States and developed a dominating empire and who did not allow outsiders to try to intrude. They were all foreign families who were close to each other. They were families like any other; however, in many of them, the father was a famous Italian mobster.

Among all the mobsters, I especially remember one the kids admired the most. He was known as Pappi, if I remember right. We admired him because at our age, having money, women, and cars represented everything, and he had all of that and more.

Everything seemed complicated. I was not able to understand all the medical and health issues the doctors and adults discussed. At home, we were not in a financial situation to pay for medical services at home or hire a nurse to provide the services we were looking for. I was adrift and without a direction to guide me as to what I should do to become a good member of society.

We didn't have much money at home. We used to clip coupons from the newspaper to buy food, we didn't go to restaurants, and it was always the same, lacking something. I was tired of all the misery and wanted to be like the other kids who had mobster fathers, had expensive stuff, and rode in cars with girls. It was such a critical situation back home that many times, we stole things we needed or wanted. I decided I was going to have my own money—real money.

I used to deliver marijuana, but that was child's play from the past, and that money was not enough to impress the girls. I had to change that. The time had come to put all those childish things aside and move on to the next level, to adult things that would lead me to a better situation.

There were several occasions when I thought it was time to go up to the next level to earn more, but it was always just a thought; I did nothing about it. The reason was unknown—maybe it was fear or a lack of balls, or maybe I was just waiting for someone or something to push me into the decision. That was the only thing I was lacking: encouragement.

Ultimately, what encouraged me was the situation at home. It was not something new, but eventually, it was the trigger and the spark that set in me the decision to go out and start doing bad things. I was only thirteen years old when I decided to commit bigger crimes.

My mother's health conditions did not improve, and the family was always concerned about her and doing our best to support her. My mom's health condition was worsening every day. Fortunately, someone was at home at that time and was able to notice it, and she was able to avoid a family tragedy.

The gang I joined was the family where I found backup, identity, and the familiar feeling I didn't find in my home, where I only heard yelling and constant complaints. My friends from the gang, who were also from the neighborhood, always understood me because they were living in the same situation I was.

The rest of the gang members had committed some crimes in the community and had some experience. Soon it was my first night. I left home without saying a word. I don't think my family even noticed that I wasn't there. Everyone was submerged in his or her own world and waiting for my mom to improve.

I met my friends, and we started walking around the neighborhood, looking for something to do. Then we went other places a little farther away where people did not recognize us and where we could leave our mark. We wanted to be recognized and earn respect.

We arrived at a corner where there was a gas station. A guy got out of his car and went into the store to buy some stuff. One of my friends followed him inside to watch him and to warn us in case he decided to leave unexpectedly.

A member of the group ran toward the car and tried to open one of the doors, but it was locked. He gave me a sign to try to open a door on the other side of the car. Without hesitation, I tried the driver's door.

Surprisingly, it was unlocked. I made a sign to tell him the door was open, and he jumped over the hood of the car, landed next to me, and, while opening the driver's door, told me, "Get in!" I opened the back door, and in the blink of an eye, we were driving away from the gas station.

Two blocks down, the group member who had been watching the driver inside the store was waiting for us.

Of course, we had other opportunities to do the same.

Paradoxically, stealing cars was not a way to earn as much money as I initially thought. There were other businesses that generated more profits, and one of those would be my next step. I didn't want to steal cars forever, because I had other objectives that were clear: I wanted to have lot of money and be admired like the Italian mobsters from my neighborhood. The $200 or $300 per robbery was not flashy enough to keep me stealing cars. But I knew I had to do it for a while to keep growing and gain more experience.

I also had to keep in mind the principles of seniority and skill. I had to wait my turn. If I rushed, I risked losing everything I had earned or losing my life if I didn't react in a calm, cautious, and smart way.

I wanted to be part of something and to feel important and valuable, and I thought crime was the way to achieve it. It seemed that was the norm among the teens and guys from the neighborhood. That was the legacy the Italian mobsters were leaving behind. It was the cursed legacy all of us boys were fighting for and trying to be part of.

It didn't matter what had to be done; the important thing was to do it and do it right to earn respect, fame, and the approval of the big bosses. In their eyes, we had to be dedicated, intrepid, and brave and, of course, keep our mouths shut, which was a silent condition we all knew well before starting off in the criminal streets.

Months were passing by, I had been in car theft for some time, and I thought I had gained some experience. However, even the most experienced doctors die.

7

THE BARS—DAMN BARS!

The engine sounded and backfired so loudly that it could be heard from far away. That drew the attention of my friends and me, and we wanted to know what was going on, so we left school and went straight to the street where the noise was coming from. My buddies knew what was going on, and from the beginning, they had been giving me hints about what they intended to do.

To our surprise, the noise was closer than we imagined, or at least we thought. In the strip mall just fifteen minutes away from home, we saw a red sports car driven by a beautiful and elegant blonde. She looked to be about forty-five years old, but despite being an older woman, she was in good shape, and without a doubt, it would have been a great experience for a fifteen-year-old boy like me. That was what I thought. But for my friends, that spectacular sports car was the first and last thought.

We chased the owner of that car for several days. She was the new owner of a luxurious store in the mall, and we calculated she lived thirty-five minutes away from her work. She always took the same route to work. We planned how to steal the car from her. I say *we* planned it because I was with them, but the reality was different. I only went with them on the outings; I didn't plan them.

We knew the only chance was in the evening, right before dark, when all the employees finished their shifts and when the traffic was not as heavy. The clock read 7:38 p.m. on that fall Thursday. We had spoken with two other members of the gang who would go with us and help us on the job. We knew it was not going to be easy, because there were several complications we had to pay close attention to, and in order to achieve our goal, we needed several trustworthy guys. While another guy and I were watching the owner of the car and the other merchants and visitors, the other members of the group were in the parking lot, surrounding the red sports car. We assumed the car would have an alarm, and we had to deactivate it before opening it.

My friend took out a key specially made to steal cars and put it in the car's lock, but nothing happened. He tried again and again—nothing. Another guy tried the other door, but he didn't have any luck either.

The image of my mother crossed my mind and distracted me for a moment, but I recovered and followed the movements of everyone in the mall.

My friend tried the key again, and all of a sudden, he could open the passenger door. The alarm only made a short beep, and my other friend immediately opened the driver's door from the side he was on. Immediately, he jumped inside the car, pulled out the wires, and connected them so he could start it and escape. They both jumped into the car and took off like bats out of hell, scared but satisfied in our success.

The other lookout and I were still making rounds in the mall. We hadn't noticed that they had left, since we had to stay with the plan. When the time was up, we left the shopping center from the exit opposite where the car had been parked and went to the place we had previously agreed on.

The fright and uncertainty began to take hold of me. I had no idea of the outcome of our adventure, but something was obvious: the others had not been caught, because when we left, we did not see any police or any activity indicating that something strange had happened, so I thought we had completed the mission.

In my mind, I started to see the green bills in my wallet. For this car, the buyers would pay us well. My friends were waiting for us. We all climbed inside the car and continued on our way, according to the plan.

Thirty minutes had passed since we left the mall. We were driving through the streets of a poor neighborhood, when we started to see colored lights everywhere. Almost simultaneously, the image of my mother came into my head again. The lights seemed familiar to me. They reminded me of the last time I had been in the hospital, when my mother had been hospitalized. While I had been in the ER, police cars, fire trucks, and ambulances had come in and out, carrying patients and sick people. Many of the patients had had accidents in the streets.

Due to my mother's constant visits to hospitals, I had to stay with my grandparents on several occasions. That was something I didn't enjoy much, especially when my grandfather spoke to me about God and getting away from the streets.

The lights and sirens came closer and closer, and as we turned the corner, two police cars were closing the road, as if they knew we were going to drive through there. Three officers made us stop and get out of the car with our hands up.

Our red-car fever was expensive. Suddenly, they were fingerprinting me in the police station for car theft. Without a doubt, at fifteen years old, I was going to be incarcerated.

The truth is, I wasn't worried about what people would say at school or back home. Three days after my incarceration, I was out and going home. I had to be good and behave because they released me on probation. I would have a supervisor bothering me anytime he wanted to, a guy breathing down my neck like my own shadow. I had to come up with a plan to free myself of this heavy burden.

8

MY NEIGHBORHOOD

The neighborhood I grew up in was violent. I suppose there are many people who have no idea how life was in that part of the United States and how youngsters like us had to deal with difficult and unsafe situations. On many occasions, my life itself was in danger. At least young men like us could defend ourselves. Imagine the situation of those who could not defend themselves or run, like children, women, and the elderly.

It would be worthwhile to clarify a bit about this. That area was famous for the Mafia, violence, deaths, drugs, and crimes committed in a period of the history of the United States. We must also understand the legacy those gangsters generated and left for future generations, without counting the widows, orphans, drug addicts, and those who died.

I think many people throughout the world have had the opportunity to see and enjoy films produced about the raw and cruel reality that area generated nationwide. My neighborhood was a typical neighborhood back then. We believed that seeing crime in the streets was normal, and we participated. It was the heritage of the criminals we wanted to imitate, whom we admired.

Criminal activities were normal in that neighborhood. All businesses had to pay to exist, to open and to sell, and for me, that was normal.

My job, and the job of many of my friends, was to collect money from the owners so they were able to exercise the right to have a business. Collecting that money was what we did every day, and a lot of people did it; it was not just us. There were different gangs who exercised that power in different areas, and each of them had different rules, taxes, teams, and collectors. It was a well-defined system in which all had their own clear roles and knew what they could and couldn't do.

The Godfather, The Untouchables, Goodfellas, and many more films depict the reality of the crime situation in those streets. Those adapted versions, in many ways, are far from the reality of people like me who lived there and have a clear understanding in their minds and hearts of the truth.

However, what we see in those movies is as close as possible to what was happening in my neighborhood. If you do not know of or haven't seen these films, let me clarify that the characters are famous members of the Mafia, which reigned for many years and committed the worst crimes possible in neighborhoods in many states of the country.

As I said, there were few things that really caught my attention and that I spent time doing. I played soccer and basketball, but if I was not doing sports, then I was involved in things that were not good or positive. That is the way I see it now because I changed, but back then, I thought that behavior was normal, was what everyone was doing, and was surely what future generations would do. I knew it was bad and negative and was a crime, but I considered it normal because everyone did it.

Sometimes I remember myself as a youngster, and I transport myself to back then. I don't see anyone—a guide, counselor, mentor, or other person—who would advise me and teach me that what I was doing was bad and criminal. I had no one close to me who could help me get out of that circle of influence, that lifestyle, and that cursed cycle.

To my misfortune, I had no mother or father to guide me in those matters.

I got into a lot of trouble with the law, which caused me great pain. I thought I was going to die before my eighteenth birthday, just as several of my friends and relatives did. Today, being a mature, professional, married father and businessman, I can assure you that I don't miss anything at all about those times, but I do keep the experiences, mistakes, triumphs, and, above all, lessons learned through my efforts and sacrifices.

I am aware that a young man of that time should be punished for the mistakes he made and bad things he did and should somehow pay for the crimes he committed. I paid the consequences; I was not an exception. I was in jail, and that is the worst thing that can happen to any human being. Being deprived of freedom and locked within four walls marked me for the rest of my life in a deep and unique way. My time there taught me in the worst way, by force, that I was not going anywhere and that my life was on a precipice, hanging by a thread so thin and weak that I could hardly stay afloat.

Despite what I'd thought I had, at the end, I had nothing. For the people I had contact with in the streets, my life was worthless. They cared only as long as I was useful. I was wasting my life, and if I didn't change my way, I would end up in a bad way or maybe even dead, which, as I said, I was sure was going to happen before my eighteenth birthday.

I'd had that thought since I was little. I was convinced I was going to be one of the greatest and most famous gangsters who ever existed, just like the ones from my neighborhood streets whom I admired. I am going to confess something: the first time I touched a firearm, I was nine years old. But that was normal in the environment I lived in. All of us wanted to be like those who walked around our streets as if they owned the whole world. Undoubtedly, those were hard times for me as well as for the other kids of my generation who directly or indirectly had to be involved with all those situations and experiences.

I am a gringo, as my Latino friends used to describe me. I grew up in a world full of African descendants, Latinos, and Italians, and because of that, I don't understand why there are people who are treated differently from each other. Why do some people treat others differently because of their skin color, their money, and so on? I am convinced that all human beings are equal by nature. God made us equal, and he did not say, "I make you different from this one and that one and that other one." No, he made us equal, regardless of any physical or material difference. That's why I don't understand why there are people who treat others differently according to what they are or have or, on the contrary, what they are not or do not have.

I treat everyone equally. I have managed many offices and people, and I work with people of all kinds, characteristics, backgrounds, and origins. To understand everyone, I treat them all with the same respect, equality, and warmth every time I talk to and interact with them. This is part of what my life has been and is a result of the difficulties, studies, experiences, achievements, and maturity that have made me an excellent human being full of virtues and teachings to share with my fellow people, as well as a connoisseur of my defects and weaknesses, which I try to manage and improve whenever I can in the best way possible. In addition, I always learn from what I do, from triumphs and failures. Of course, what I learn from people is something immeasurable and impressive.

Not everything that went on in my neighborhood was bad or a crime. There were moments of fun, friendship, and great times, as well as time for friends, family, and love. As a teenager, love came to me from an Italian girl whom I loved a lot and with whom I shared almost seven years. It was a nice relationship from which I learned a lot and which I keep as a beautiful memory.

Among my most outstanding memories is that of the graduation party and prom I went to with my girlfriend. It was a spectacular party, and all my friends and I looked elegant and beautiful. We looked so different and so distinguished that we looked like TV celebrities. I danced and had fun the whole time the party lasted. It was sensational to be able to share that special date with special people at that stage of my life, even though I never stood out for being a good student. I think I excelled at being a great athlete, which I liked and which distinguished me from the group.

There were many celebrations shared with my girlfriend, my family, and my friends. As in any normal family, I have special memories of birthday celebrations, where I always ate cake and had lots of fun. My brother and sisters were always there to share the occasion and make those special moments unforgettable.

Those moments are ones I hope to keep forever in my life, when all the people I loved the most would gather around a table in a room to share, talk, eat, celebrate, and laugh without any commitment other than being a united family full of love.

9

THE SPORTS

Scoring and keeping scoring to stay ahead and succeed in life

One of my biggest passions was sports. I practiced every day. Since I was a good soccer player when I was in high school, people came from universities to watch me play, and several offered me the opportunity to study and play with them. My habit was to play with people older than I was, and maybe that's why I stood out—not that the others were elderly, but they were a few years older. During high school, I traveled with universities because they wanted to take me to play and study with them. I took many trips through different states and cities in the United States, all thanks to soccer. They were nice times.

But despite the offers from universities, the lack of family principles and support and advice from an adult and all the negative and bad things I had done so far outweighed the sports and offers from universities. From that moment on, the most difficult things in my life were about to come. I was still a clueless, beardless young man who didn't have a base or a coach to support me and advise me, someone who would serve as a positive example to get out of that criminal world. I had no one to encourage me to follow a different path with some of the universities opening their doors to me by doing something I loved: playing soccer. Unfortunately, I kept making mistakes.

I participated in several soccer championships, representing schools at the national and state levels, always demonstrating great ball-handling skills and being a natural scorer in each match. To this day, I still have a lot of ability on the field, and of course, I have indelible memories, along with old newspaper clippings in which my accomplishments were written about in an almost fantastical way, born from the colorful imagination of a Hollywood writer.

Every morning, I used to leave early to run, practice soccer, or play any sport. That was a daily discipline, no matter the weather or anything else. I love sports and all physical activity, and I am always looking to do something, some movement, but never indoors. That is something I can't stand.

Sports have been an integral part of my life and my development. I did not have a counselor when I was young to help me make wiser decisions at that time. Today I think I lost the opportunity to develop a sport at a professional level, which surely would have been soccer.

I feel that physical conditioning and sports in general help you in many different ways. They not only keep you physically well but also help you to destress, cleanse your body, remove impurities, and keep your mind and your attitude awake and alert. All of these are important factors in the development of a person.

If we look at sports as mental and psychological help to get away from and keep people away from vices, drugs, bad thoughts, and bad activities, we can see that it would be worthwhile for all human beings to practice some kind of physical activity or sport.

I have the opportunity to sponsor and support some teams and youngsters in their commitment to sports. Fortunately, many of them have emerged triumphant and won their respective leagues and championships. In addition, I enjoy the privilege of supporting some local soccer leagues in which the sport of soccer and the well-being of our community are being fostered.

Practice sports. It's one of the best alternatives to cure any illness and suffering, even diseases of the soul and the heart.

10

AGAIN, JAIL

One time, a gang member asked me to do him the favor of keeping a package in my school locker. I did it without hesitation. I put the package he gave me inside my locker with my notebooks and pens. The flaw was that I didn't notice there were people around watching the package and my suspicious behavior. I was aware of the contents of the package I was keeping in my locker. However, I never imagined that someone was going to rat me out to the authorities.

It was about ten o'clock in the morning on a hot day in May, when the principal of the school knocked on the door of my classroom and immediately opened it without waiting for permission to enter. He looked around and called my name. My first reaction was as if I felt an electrical shock all over my body. *The package!* I thought immediately.

As I left the room, I was full of fear but showed a quiet and audacious brazenness on the outside. The principal didn't utter a single word as we walked to my locker. As we turned to the hall a few steps before reaching my locker, I saw that two police officers were waiting to open it. Once we arrived, without asking, they opened the locker, and they found the package, which would represent many legal problems, including being arrested, taken to jail, and locked up for a week. The five weapons found in my locker were enough evidence of a crime, and although they were not my weapons, I was responsible for them. After a week in prison, I was able to get out on probation.

Today I wonder how someone can be so foolish and innocent—or maybe it's just the teenage hormones—to think and feel that he is invincible and that nothing negative or bad can ever happen to him. In my case, despite being locked up and on probation, I didn't stop doing things or getting involved in things that, in the end, represented more trouble in my life. Even just hanging with people who were involved in the same things represented a latent risk of getting into trouble.

One day, while I was still on probation, other people I was hanging out with committed a crime. I was with my friends, and I was arrested again. I was still on probation, so things got much more complicated for me, and all just for being in the wrong place at the wrong time. Again, prison was my destiny; I was arrested again. At that time, I told myself, *This is what bad things do—bad friendships, bad decisions, and, of course, not having someone to advise you, scold you, and tell you, "No! Enough! No more mistakes."* On the contrary, what I had in my environment were people who pushed me and encouraged me to get into more and more trouble and into more criminal and illegal situations.

I felt sad about these things, because at eighteen years old, I was losing my freedom again, and that is something precious. Nobody who hasn't experienced prison can imagine the magnitude of that situation— the despair, sadness, nostalgia, and anger.

Now the situation would have another cost, as I was eighteen years old. The young sports lover who had traveled to represent several universities now was a man, one who, in his hard and solitary life without counselors, had lost his freedom again.

To my misfortune, on that occasion, the arrest was in the high school in New Jersey. I had always wanted to go to college and play soccer, but I didn't think I ever could under those circumstances. I didn't believe I was going to go to prison, but they arrested me at school with a firearm.

Nevertheless, with the sufferings and difficulties in that prison, I had a lot of time to think, reconsider, and shape what my future would be. I faced an uncertain future because I didn't know how to do anything. I only knew about sports and crimes. While in prison, I concluded that I had to make a change in my life—a total and absolute change forever. It was clear that if I continued like this, I would not get anywhere good and surely would end up dead or getting a much longer sentence for something even more serious.

My time inside the walls of that prison in New Jersey helped me a lot to think and reflect. My life was in chaos, a waste. It had neither beginning nor end. I was wasting my life. I had thrown it into a garbage dump for a long time, but that had to change. I had to change; it was my obligation and my commitment. In order to change, I had to start immediately and not let anything or anyone change or alter my decision.

Early the next day, I started my change. While locked up, I started many studies. I learned how to use computers of that era and learned accounting. I improved my Spanish a little and learned many other things that, throughout my personal and professional life, have been of great help.

While in prison, I often remembered my friend who'd died at sixteen years old. He had been still a child and had been a good friend. When he'd died, I'd asked myself, *Will I make it to eighteen?* When I was eighteen and locked in there, I thought, *Will I make it to twenty-one?* That thought kept me up at night because in prison, no one knows what, when, or where things will happen. What the inmates know for sure is that something will happen. In prison, you see everything: rapes, drugs, crimes, and people who use prison as a hotel. They come and go, and a short time later, they are back. Many of them are just messengers or bodyguards who have to commit a crime to be locked up again so they can keep taking care of their bosses. That was something really crazy.

Life in prison is not easy for anyone, not even for those who think they are very brave. Imprisonment leaves marks on absolutely everyone. Time runs slowly when you are locked up. Months, weeks, days, hours, minutes, and even seconds are counted. The notion of dates and celebrations gets lost. That is the time in incarceration. But luckily, it happens without giving us a chance to return.

It eventually was time to end my sentence, and the doors of the jail seemed so close but, at the same time, so far away that I could not believe it. I had mixed feelings: happiness for my freedom and sadness I left inside. I left prison with a clear and well-defined idea to change, but there outside, I asked myself, "How?"

But God's plans are great and immeasurable. Out of nowhere, my grandfather appeared, and it was he who gave me that last push to change. He told me that what I had to do was change. I remember his words as if it were yesterday. I had grown up in a difficult world full of evil and crime, and I had been alone and without a guide, but it was time to change. That was the moment when all the negatives became positive. It didn't matter what had surrounded me before. I knew that lifestyle was bad, and if I continued like that, I was always going to have problems.

It was obvious I had to change completely and leave behind in the past any contact, as small as it might have been, with that world I had grown up in. I started making a radical change in my life. I didn't want to go back to that environment in my neighborhood and with my friends, and to that end, my decision was to stay in New Jersey and not come back home.

Afterward, things seemed to start to have another color for my future—a color that at times seemed dark and didn't show anything positive. However, I assumed that darkness as a personal challenge I had to change and overcome to get ahead.

I knew beforehand that things would not be easy or simple and that I had to fight hard to subsist and survive. Life in New Jersey was not easy. It was necessary to get a job to pay the bills, but one job was not enough because money was short, so I had to get two full-time jobs to subsist and make ends meet. I invested almost all my time in that. The rest I used to rest and to study computer science in a school that was close by. I had all my hopes and expectations set that such change was going to be positive in my life and in my future.

11

TIME TO CHANGE

Now that time has passed and a lot of water has gone under the bridge, I can say with certainty that experiences only help if we take the good from them. It is worthless if you live through many experiences and don't learn from them. As a man who has walked many different paths, I can assure you it is never too late to get on the right path and do the right things. You form your own destiny with your decisions and actions, and whatever you decide will impact your future and, believe it or not, also the futures of the people who surround you. There are many human beings who, even if you have no idea, look up to you as an example and wish they were like you. You are the mirror they would like to see their reflection in, and their futures depend upon your decisions and actions.

Remember, all jobs are honorable. It might not be the most positive one, but it's your job, and if you already have it, do it right. But think deeply about whether or not that is what you really wish to do. If it is what you want to do, invest your life and time in it, so in the end, you don't feel as if you have wasted valuable time. If you decide it is not what you want to do, then stop, adjust, and change your path and direction if necessary. Redirect your course, but don't abandon your future, your destiny, or your development. It's human to reassess and adjust but not to desist and give up. Remember the poem at the beginning of this book.

One of the jobs I had in New Jersey was at a scrap metal company. It was a hard and heavy job where I had to give it all for a salary that didn't justify all the work that had to be done, but I gave my word, and I felt the commitment. I had a commitment, and I was not going to give up just because the job was hard and different from what I was used to.

In that job, I had to clean, receive, and work with metals and cans all day. My body and my clothes were dirty and stained black almost all day. I used to sweat like a horse and smell even worse. My shift started early in the morning. At five o'clock in the morning, I had to already have my hands in the scrap, and at four o'clock in the afternoon, when my shift was over, I was almost breathless and fatigued from the workday.

But I knew I couldn't waste my time or be lazy, because I had another commitment. After my shift at the scrap company, I went to a fast food restaurant to keep working and earn more money to pay my bills. By the time my shift was over, it was already night. I ran to my house to try to rest, but I knew beforehand that my day was not over. If I wanted to get ahead, I had to make more sacrifices. At home, my journey of personal growth and intellectual formation was waiting for me via my online classes.

Many times, thoughts and memories of my life in Philadelphia crossed my mind. I even wanted to return. I came close to taking my few things and returning to my world, the world that I wanted to leave but that stubbornly seemed to condemn me to return.

I think that if I had not been clear about what I did and didn't want, I would not be writing this, and I would never have become the person I am today. I was convinced of what I wanted. I was determined to achieve it at any cost. Those first sacrifices were the ones that had to be made to get ahead and leave behind once and for all my dark past of gang life.

One day, at my scrap job, a man came to throw away a couple of old lawnmowers. I asked him why he was throwing them away, and he said that their life cycle was over and that his job demanded new tools in order to be accomplished, due to the quantity and quality of the work his company had to deliver.

That chat clicked inside my head. I began to pay attention to the lawns on my way to work, and I noticed that many of them were neglected, untidy, and in appalling condition.

On the contrary, in other areas of the city, there were many neighborhoods where the yards were so spectacular that they seemed ready for a contest. Those gardens were maintained and cared for by companies like the one owned by the man from the junkyard.

Once, I stopped at one of those yards and asked one of the workers about the work. I was surprised by his response. He told me that the business he worked for was busy and that his boss was hiring staff practically every day. He told me there were many people who paid well for their yards to be maintained. I asked him if he knew how much his boss charged to take care of those yards. He couldn't give me an exact number, but he gave me an approximate. Then I asked him, "How much do you earn to cut this grass?"

He said, "I get paid by the day. I don't know how many yards I do—as many as my boss tells me."

An idea came to my mind.

After a few days of thinking about it, I made my decision: I would start my first company, a landscaping company.

I didn't quit my job. I bought a pickup truck with my savings, and I hired a person to do the job while I was at work. It wasn't easy, but it wasn't impossible either.

I started from scratch, saving every cent and not wasting my money. I moved forward with patience, intelligence, persistence, faith, and the belief that I was going to succeed without harming others.

It was somehow the test of fire to prove to myself that by doing good, you get a good reward back, and by surrounding yourself with good people, you get good results. Besides, now I not only was an entrepreneur but also was giving work to other people who depended on me and trusted me.

Life was changing for the better, and I was the architect of that change.

12

TAKE ADVANTAGE OF THE OPPORTUNITIES AND THE TIME

When you grow up on the streets, you learn to defend yourself, think as people on the streets do, and maneuver along the most tangled and complicated roads. On the streets, you learn big-time survival strategies, strengths that others do not have to develop, a different sense of seeing things, and an ability to take advantage of any given opportunity. That was exactly what I wanted to develop in my life: the use of every good and positive opportunity I saw around me. It is amazing how many things you can do, how much work there is to do, and how much money you can earn if you only think positive and, even more important, get into action.

I remember the words of a book that say, more or less, "Every thought not followed by an action is completely useless." This is true.

Every thought we have and everything we plan, we have to take it into action. Otherwise, those plans will be just ideas and thoughts. Maybe they're great and well-planned projects, but they will be nothing more, which, in the end, means junk. A plan means nothing if you don't put it to work in practice. That was exactly what I intended to start to do in my life: make things happen.

I knew in advance that it would not be simple and perhaps would be expensive in terms of money and time, but I would make all the sacrifices necessary to achieve and fulfill my goals and objectives.

It was clear to me from all I had learned on the streets, in prison, and in business that I had to get the most of all my physical and intellectual potential and turn everything into something positive to transform my life and future and have the freedom to keep winning and growing.

My landscaping company grew slowly. Due to my other jobs, it was hard to have enough time to invest in it; however, I still had it, and I was more persistent each day. I was sure the jobs I was doing for others would not last forever because, among other things, I didn't want it that way.

I still had the idea in my head that one has to do something that lasts forever and not just simple things that maybe fill up your stomach at the moment but oblige you to think about how to fill it up tomorrow. I didn't want to keep with that poor and small mentality; I had to think bigger and be conscious that in the business world, there are always people trying to take advantage and trying to find the right moment to make a fool of us and take away what we deserve and what we worked for. I didn't want to go through those situations again.

With that clear objective in my head, I kept working hard day to day, saving and trying hard daily. In my mind, I believed that if I was good at stealing cars and delivering marijuana, drugs, and firearms, I should be even better at developing my own project and my own company and helping others to get ahead. Why not help kids who were just like I was, the ones who couldn't see the light at the end of the tunnel?

I kept working hard steadily for a long time. I didn't quit or slow down, although on many occasions, I felt as if I were failing in my attempt. But my desire to excel and succeed was much stronger and didn't let me break down, although I was about to give up and leave everything to return to a life that had given me the expectation that I would die before I was eighteen years old. But I was doing something that I believed was good and that people believed was good, and again, my uncle's words echoed in my head and made me react. I had to change the negative into positive and do something that had sense and significance in my life. Did I want to keep being a waste, or did I want to get ahead and be successful and productive? I knew the answer beforehand, so I kept working and fighting for what I wanted.

13

ALWAYS WITH GOD BY MY SIDE

There is someone I have not talked about yet: God. It sounds funny or even paradoxical that someone inside the criminal world would mention God, but I have to do it. I have to do it because with time, I discovered that God has always been by my side. He has always accompanied me.

When I lived on the streets of my city and New Jersey, I wasn't killed. The times I went to prison were for short periods of time, and I came out in good shape. Fortunately, I never tried to kill another person, and my being still alive and having the desire to improve is definitely because God was with me. I didn't falter because God, from all his enormity, gave me a reason every day to move forward and understand that things were going to change for the better. But everything has its time and place, and I had to wait for mine.

A sign of the greatness of the Almighty was about to come. Opportunities should be taken when they come and not later.

God put someone in my path who was going to test the knowledge acquired in the studies I did during my stay in the prison in New Jersey and after my work at the fast food restaurant. I was beginning to see that those long journeys I'd felt were never ending would begin to bear fruit. That was God's plan.

That was how I met a businessman, a successful merchant whom people admired a lot. We talked for some time, mostly discussing general interest topics, until one day I asked him what he did for a living. Without hesitation, he told me, "Numbers and helping people."

That answer intrigued me, and I wanted to learn more about that mix. Calmly, he told me about his company, what he did, and the way his company was helping the community. He did accounting for some companies and taxes for many people. That was the way this entrepreneur made his living, and he was successful and helped people. He had a business and accounting company with twenty-three locations. It didn't take long for me to start working for him.

I didn't have much experience in that field; I only had my online night classes, and basically, I hadn't had the opportunity to apply my skills and knowledge in that field. I started by taking a tax course. Then I started doing accounting for a company. There were few taxes I managed to do that first year.

I had studied accounting and computer science, but I had no idea about taxes; I just knew they were taken away from my paycheck—that was it. My task was to learn how to do taxes, and I did. Soon I was doing taxes by hand after learning from a tax attorney.

Because I had a clear idea of what I wanted, it didn't take long to learn more about taxes and the different ways to do them. Each day, I progressed more in my knowledge within the company, and each year, the amount of taxes I did increased.

Everything learned in life, sooner or later, is useful. I never thought that knowledge would be something to be used to my advantage, but in truth, it was an important tool I had not taken advantage of as I should have.

While living in my city, as I said, I practiced many sports, especially soccer. I interacted and shared with many Latinos. They were always happy, kind, and fun. They used to joke with me. Because I didn't know how to speak Spanish, sometimes they started talking only Spanish among them, and I couldn't understand anything. Sometimes I thought they made fun of me, based on the joy they displayed. Over time, I understood that they were not making fun of me; they enjoyed soccer so much that they always laughed and were happy to play it, as well as to play it with an American who was very good at it. They wanted to make me part of their world so I would always play with them. I began to speak Spanish little by little to the point where I could communicate with all of them. I stopped thinking their laughs were because of me and started learning many things.

Due to my skills as a bilingual person and the fact that we had many Latino clients, one day my boss had a meeting with me after a brief business chat, and he made me understand how important and beneficial it would be to teach taxes in Spanish for the Latinos from our area. For me, that was unbelievable. My Spanish was bad, and I told him I hardly could have long conversations, but he winked at me as if to say, "You can do this."

Well, then I was teaching taxes in Spanish for the Latino community. My life was still changing, and I enjoyed that. I was convinced that life would give me many more successes.

Who would have thought that with my rudimentary Spanish, I would have been doing that job? I say it again: God's designs.

Days were passing by, and more and more Latinos and people from different communities came into the office to get their taxes done and to learn many more things.

Again, God and his destiny had new and positive surprises.

The manager at the office where I was working got into some situations I didn't fully understand, but the owner of the company decided to fire him. Without hesitation, the owner, the man I had met by coincidence, gave me a new opportunity: general manager for the office.

A new horizon was opening to me. This was a wonderful opportunity to demonstrate what I could do, what I was made of, and where I wanted to go.

My numbers gradually increased. The first year, I only did 130 taxes; the second year, I went up to 600; and by the third year, I was already a general manager.

The opportunity and the job as a manager opened up much more the panorama and horizon of things that can be achieved, but also, I discovered that not everything that seems to be right is really right.

I started to realize there were some internal situations in the company that I thought were not the best for the image of the company and much less for what I personally believed and felt was in the best interest of our customers.

I made a decision and spoke with my boss to let him know about the things I didn't like, including, above all, the way some people were treated in the company. That was not the idea I had about how customer service should be, much less the way I would like to be treated. Fortunately, I had the power in my hands to manage and fix many things. The customer service being provided was at a low level, and I had to do something to improve it.

After a few months acting as manager of the office and implementing some measures to improve everything in general, I thought it was time to continue with my personal plans.

I asked my boss to meet with me to have a formal conversation, and he agreed. I expressed my interest in setting up and starting my own tax and accounting business, and I asked if he could advise me, teach me, and help me to get ahead with this project. By the way he looked at me, I knew in advance his answer and thoughts.

I discovered—well, rediscovered—that there are always people who use you or to whom you are useful as long as you provide them something; otherwise, you are just another simple person who works for them.

The answer of my boss was something along the lines of "Don't get into that. It's very costly. There is a lot of money that has to be invested."

I believed him—for a while. I kept working to learn other different things I needed to but without putting aside or forgetting about my plan to open my own business. Six months after that conversation with my boss and after having learned other important things, I had a brief meeting with him and told him, "You know what? I am leaving." His answer was clear: he told me to stay with him for one more year so I wouldn't have to sign a noncompete contract, a contract that forbid me to work in the same field within a specific geographic area.

But the die was cast, and my decision was made. I opened my own business with bilingual service in Spanish and English. I was my own boss and my only employee. I did everything; there were no other employees. I was in charge of everything. Delivering flyers and business cards, I went out to talk to people about the new business and promote it face-to-face. If I didn't have clients, I went out to the streets to convince people of the advantages of my new business.

I must confess it was hard. I invested a lot in that starting effort, but it was worth it. I invested my own life there.

Starting a business is not as easy as people think or as it seems. People don't trust as easily in a new company, especially if the business is related to one's personal and confidential information and to one's money. Accounting and taxes are 100 percent related to money, and people are very private about money.

The first year with my own company, I only did sixty-five taxes. That yearly number was not enough to maintain and defray the expenses of that company. It didn't give me a margin to sustain myself and cover my own bills.

However, my effort and courage were bigger and stronger than those small numbers from that first year. I knew that I had to strengthen my strategies and efforts for the next year and that my work had to be harder. Also, I had to make some adjustments in my expenses.

In the second year, I surpassed the previous year with a new number that seemed almost magical: seven hundred. So things had another color, and the business approached another horizon of success.

In the third year, the number of taxes made exceeded 1,700, and from then on, my company always continued to exceed the numbers year after year.

14

THE ILLUSION OF A FAMILY

Maybe many of you are wondering if, during that time, I dedicated myself only to business, start-up companies, and work and didn't worry about creating spaces or time for my personal life. Well, that was not so. Those years were my beginning as an entrepreneur and also my beginning as a husband and father.

I got married when I was thirty-five years old to the woman who, at that time, fulfilled my life. Those were beautiful years that gave us two wonderful children: a boy who is twenty and a precious girl who is ten. My son was born before our marriage because his mother and I had a relationship long before that.

I come from a complicated family. My beloved mother spent a lot of her time in hospitals, my father never provided in the house, and I had to be alone in the street, making my own decisions and doing what I thought was best. There was never anyone to advise or guide me in those necessary years, and there were always people around waiting to recruit young people to get them into trouble. For those reasons, we made the decision to abandon what we had built to prevent the children from growing up in a negative environment full of bad things.

One of the strongest reasons for leaving everything was that I did not want my son to find out about my past; I wanted to keep those things with me and take them to the grave with me when the time came. Obviously, as a responsible father, I wanted, and continue to want, to keep my son and other children and young people in general from getting involved in the kind of world in which I grew up. That is mainly why we are in Virginia.

I guess many people will say that parents can control their children only at home, but outside, it is difficult or almost impossible. Even so, I wanted to do my best and do everything that was within my reach.

My son had no knowledge of his father's past and entanglement with the underworld in which I was immersed for years, practically from birth. I knew in advance that it was going to be complicated to control everything and that as my son grew up, he was going to make his own decisions, and maybe I wouldn't like many of them. But even so, I wanted to risk everything I had achieved to get my great family away from those dangers that surrounded us.

Although it was clear that my son was going to grow up and be independent, it was also clear that each and every one of us needs someone to support us, back us up, and advise us, no matter what stage of life we are living or how old we are. We all, as human beings, live different situations that take us to different moments, either complicated or happy moments, which make us need cheering words, a tap on the back, and a helping hand. I decided I would do everything in my power to provide my son with a more pleasant and dignified life, without the normal dangers of the society in which I had grown up.

After my discussing with his mother and solving many of my legal affairs and business, we made the decision to leave our place of residence and arrive at a place where we, including my son, could establish ourselves, continue being a great family, and have success in business without forgetting my commitment to the community: to help people, especially children and youths, in need who were forgotten and abandoned.

We discussed different places to go to live and decided that Virginia was our best option. We packed our belongings for our new adventure and started the journey around the year 2007.

Those first days were complicated and confusing for everyone. We arrived in an area unknown and different from what we were used to living in.

But the decision was made, and the best thing to do was to keep our heads up, develop our plans, and not give up. I started learning the city and the best places to start my job.

15

A TOTAL NEW BEGINNING

I toured the city and its nearest counties to have a clear idea of the community, their needs, and, of course, the competition that was going to be around. I discovered there were not many tax businesses that offered services in Spanish, and I realized that an accessible place close to the Latino community would be a good option to start. I also knew that many Americans would become interested in the services I was going to offer.

A few days later, I already had my own space, which I shared with a beauty salon, and I stayed there for a few months, waiting for the opportunity to take the big leap. However, things at first were not the best; the business was growing little by little, slowly. But every day, I felt that I had chosen the perfect and ideal place.

Because the initial situation didn't allow it, I didn't have any help; I started alone. Once again, I distributed business cards, made new face-to-face contacts, and talked to people about my office and the services I offered, and people listened to me.

Many Latinos saw me as an American, but when I approached them and spoke to them in Spanish, they immediately changed their attitudes and opened their doors, listening to me without any problem.

Little by little, slowly, I gained people's trust. My business started to grow, and that was how I formed my first company, which, in a short time, was recognized within the community, especially among Latinos. That was just the beginning; I still had a long way to go and a lot of taxes to do.

Over time, I hired a lady in my office who contributed a lot to the development of the company. She was a person of good principles and was good at what she did, honest, and professional. She worked with me for several years.

For a long time, with a lot of work, professionalism, honesty, and dedication to our clients, my business became the number one in the area.

Mainly, Latinos benefited from the services we provided. Of course, I earned money for my work, but they benefited in working with an honest and legitimate company that prepared taxes in the best way so that clients got the highest possible refund or, if necessary, paid as little as possible, always within the legal parameters provided by the tax laws.

Alongside the tax preparation services, the accounting services my company offered were growing. Back then, there were few companies providing Spanish tax services, and there were even fewer—almost none—dedicated to providing accounting services for the Latino businesses in the area. Normally, they had to hire a company that provided English services and then hire someone to interpret. Thanks to that, my company hit the spot among the Latino community in general.

While I was the owner of my company, I always tried to return to the community what I received as a company and as a person. Today I continue doing the same, and I will continue doing it no matter where I am.

As time went on, I had to hire more people, mainly during tax season. For those dates, the demand for our services was so great that in the office, we easily had seven people working, helping all of our clients with their questions and matters related to taxes.

The company grew to such an extent that its fame transcended local borders and reached the ears of top executives of large tax companies, the heavyweights of the national tax companies' market.

One of them, back in 2010, told one of his executives to contact me to talk about business. Their business was clear: they wanted to buy my baby, my company that had started no more than two years ago but had grown so much that they could not believe it. They could not find answers for such a huge success.

We had some meetings, almost reaching a preagreement for the sale of my company, and the conversations we had were fruitful. They were practically putting out all the conditions to make the sale and get a good profit. However, I had to give up the negotiation and temporarily forget that wonderful offer.

Many people think that when you are successful in business, then you are successful in all matters of life, but the reality is that it is not always like that.

I am a simple man without complications, so in 2009, when I got married, I did it without any reception or festivities. It was a simple ceremony and nothing else. I always tried to carry on my family life in the same way: quiet and simple but with a decent life and good living full of principles.

My children are being raised under the premises of responsibility, love, union, honesty, and sincerity. Those are things I value, and I am thankful for the people who are close to my family or part of it.

But with my bad luck and the normal life circumstances all human beings encounter and from which perhaps many people do not escape, I had family and marital problems that began to undermine the wonderful family world I had, for which I had fought tirelessly. Sometimes we forget moments and situations that undoubtedly represent much more than making a business and earning some money. You believe that business is more important because in the end, its product—money—is what will be left to our loved ones.

Well, to my surprise, that was not the reality I had at home. The reality was quite another, and in the blink of an eye, although it had been a long time coming, my wife and I were separating.

This was happening at the same time the great national company wanted to buy my firm. I was awed by that business while my family world collapsed.

But I am a man aware of my reality. I never try to lie to myself or others or to cover the sun with one finger. I finally ended up separating from my wife in 2016.

That situation caused me a lot of personal and work difficulties for some time, because it was a little hard for me to dedicate all the necessary attention to the company's matters. Only those who go through such a situation can actually express how it feels.

Fortunately, time passes and helps to heal everything and close wounds. Scars and memories remain as beautiful remembrances of shared years. During that time of separation and even after that, I reflected that in the end, everything happens at its exact moment for a reason. It reminded me that God's moments are perfect, and nothing happens without him deciding.

With those thoughts, I went ahead with my life's work, leaving behind what happened in my personal and family life and taking into consideration that this was a part of my life and that now things would be a little different.

Despite the family situation, the company continued growing without any restraint. The experience of the proposal from the national company was in the past, and although it could have been a wonderful opportunity to make a small fortune and continue my expansion to other territories, I knew well that if God decided so, I would surely have a new opportunity that might be better.

During those years, my company was considered the number-one tax company among the Latino community. We no longer only offered tax services, but we developed a series of services, such as notary service, payroll preparation, and accounting for companies, among others.

Each day I realized that when a person really wants a change in his or her life, he or she works to achieve it, and if he or she also has clear and achievable objectives and does not give up, there is no doubt success will be at the end of the road.

It might sound easy, but it's really not. However, it is not impossible. As I said, you have to have clear and defined thoughts and get them into action to achieve them.

People should have a life plan and follow it to the letter. You can start with small objectives; they do not necessarily have to involve big companies and achievements. Everything has to go step by step to the extent of our capabilities and possibilities.

It is not advisable to plan large objectives at the beginning, because if they cannot be achieved, they can create a huge disappointment in people. This does not mean we cannot have giant projects for our future; it simply means we must start with small achievements and gradually increase the size and complexity of them.

I would like to give you a simple example. If you want to have a house, it would be advisable to think of a small house tailored to your needs. Do not think of a big mansion full of rooms, bathrooms, patios, and many other things. The best thing to do is to think about a house that meets your initial basic needs, and once you get that model home, after enjoying it for a while, then it might be time to think about changing it for a new and better one. Just like that, slowly but surely, keep working without stopping until you get the big house you wanted from the beginning.

You can have great thoughts for your future, and that is wonderful, but you have to keep in mind that everything is achieved step by step by calmly working hard with persistence, dedication, honesty, love, and faith in God. You can be sure that on that road, there will be many moments when you feel like dying and you want to give up, leave everything aside, and go back to your past. All of that is normal and is part of the process.

The most important thing is to know that this is going to happen and is normal; it is something that has to be lived, experienced, and overcome. Also, there will be times when you believe that nothing comes out the way you want it to or that the stars and the universe are allied against you. A number of negative experiences will lead you to think it is best to give up and kill each of your projects. Maybe that is the time to stop, rest, rethink, and adjust your goals, your plans, and the way you are working to achieve each of them.

There is nothing wrong with stopping, adjusting, and rethinking. Nobody has the magic formula for success. The shot of luck and prosperity doesn't exist. Success is achieved only with hard work, study, and dedication. So when you feel yourself fall, just stop for a moment, look at everything you have achieved and how far you have come, and verify that your goals and objectives are real and can be achieved with the plan you developed.

If you have to make changes or adjustments to your objectives, do it without fear and without hesitation. It is better to make those adjustments as you go than to arrive at the faked end of success, meaning you think you've achieved your goal, but in reality, it's just an optical illusion, a disguised reality, a lying dream that will turn into a sad nightmare.

That's what I've done in my own life. Not everything has been easy. There have been many times when things have not gone the way I proposed or planned them. When that has happened, I have had to stop and think about what to do, what would be the best option, and the way in which I should adjust or change my plans to achieve success and the desired goals. It is in those moments when you have to be at the top, because it is important to be at 100 percent and have all the thoughts at the highest level to take the most appropriate new measures to get where you want.

Later, I will talk a little more about this process and how anyone can be successful. I always tell myself that if I, a person who lived in crime and did negative things, could come from where I have and have the plans that I have, why can't other people be successful and achieve everything that is proposed in life?

16

LIFE AND SUCCESS DO NOT WAIT

After the separation from my ex-wife, difficult times came into my life, despite the fact that my business continued growing, and other businesses remained afloat with relative success.

There were many moments when I wanted to stop everything and stay with what I had achieved until then, but something inside me told me that was not the best and that no matter how complicated the circumstances I was going through at the time were, everything was going to happen, and the waters would return to their normal course.

With all those thoughts in my head and a clear mind, I decided the best way was to keep going with my plans. I knew that what had happened with my family was part of my past, but they would keep being part of my present and my future, and my children would never be alone. My father was never at home, and I was not going to do the same, even when we were not living under the same roof.

My business brand was growing each day, and each tax season, more and more people contacted us to trust us with their taxes, and by then, many companies trusted their payrolls to our hands.

As we grew as a company, other companies started to operate in the market, some disappeared, and some were also growing. The market of people in need of tax preparation became increasingly larger and more demanding; therefore, new companies entered the competition, which forced us to provide a better and more professional service every day.

One of the new companies in the market was a large company with tentacles nationwide, which made it an unfair competition by its size, its ability to move, and the money it had for its development. It was the little sister of what was considered the largest tax company in the United States.

The original company is a leading company nationwide in the area of taxes, especially among the English-speaking market. Its tentacles even reach other countries, where it has several offices. Its owner has many years of experience in that field; he is skilled and has the necessary knowledge to develop many companies at any level.

After many market studies and many discussions, that company decided to open a sister company dedicated to attack the Latin market in the tax field.

My company continued with its great work, developing each of its plans to attend to and assist the community in general. We were clear that nothing and no one, not even the biggest companies, would make us withdraw from the market. We were clear on what we wanted and where we wanted to go.

Obviously, we were aware that each day would be more difficult, and maybe we would have to make adjustments or changes, but we would not give up on our work.

The other great company, in its effort to cover all markets, contacted me because they wanted to talk to me. After some attempts, we finally agreed and scheduled what would be the first of many meetings. The owner of the other two companies was the host of the meetings. As I mentioned before, he is a wise man with broad experience and is capable of accomplishing almost anything. His power is such that he is ranked as one of the most influential businessmen in the United States.

Well, after several talks and explanations of the purpose of their companies, the main focus of the conversation came up: the commercial proposal they had planned meticulously.

They were clear in explaining to me that what they wanted and were looking for was my company. They had been following my company. They knew almost every commercial movement I had made, and they had information regarding my business, my employees, and the services we provided. They knew almost everything about my company, to say the least.

They expressed their interest in buying my company. My small company was on the radar of what I thought was the largest and most important tax company in the United States.

Even with all that presentation, my initial response was a no. I said, "No, I don't want to. I love my company, and I already had a proposal of this nature made by another company." The situation brought back memories of the conversation I'd had with the other company and what I'd been going through at that time in my personal life.

They insisted and showed me a lot more about their company, their philosophy, the plans they had for the Latino community, and the benefits the deal would bring for me and my employees.

The meeting was longer than expected, but I think it was necessary because there was a lot at stake.

I felt the deal could be the great opportunity I had been waiting for to grow and fulfill my dreams and plans, or it could become a catastrophe that led me to failure. *Failure* was a word that I knew existed but that had never been in my thoughts, as if I had erased it from my own dictionary.

I analyzed the offer for many days, and I consulted with several people. It is not wrong or a crime to ask for advice when you are not sure what has to be done, especially if you are not sure what can happen.

Plus, it is well known that several heads think better than one, and there are intelligent people with other ways of thinking and analyzing situations.

Many thoughts went through my head from the days when I'd delivered marijuana, my days in prison, my work in the scrap metal company, and my success with my current company, but now I would be getting into a business that could give me a lot or maybe get me out of the market. But I knew that if God had put this test in my way, it was because he had it predisposed. Again, God's timing is perfect.

So after learning about the other company's vision, consulting with several people, and convincing myself that this opportunity was sent by God, I accepted the offer and the sale conditions.

The other company's owner and I knew well that the Latino community would become the largest one in the United States with their acquisition and investing power. The quantity of money that community would be managing would be large, and for that reason, it was important to have solid bases to reach it.

Among the proposals they offered was not just for them to buy my company but for me to become part of the new different company. My job position would be as a vice president on a national level.

That position got my attention because I considered that from there, I could continue working on what I liked, but I would also have the chance to help the Latinos from different fronts. That was something I wanted to develop from within the great commercial monster.

My life was now divided between different cities in the United States. The job kept me traveling and in meetings constantly. I continued to learn about companies, personnel management, and accounting. I met important people who moved in large spheres, and of course, I opened new locations of the new company brand.

My direct boss was a woman with a lot of sales experience but apparently little experience in taxes and personnel management. I tried to do everything possible to learn that world, but as a president, there are no chances for gaps, let alone letting your subordinates know you don't know the answers or the way to make a business or a proposal or simply giving an erroneous answer that, for a person who manages the world of taxes, would be something supremely easy and simple.

A few months after I started with that company as a vice president, having done a great job, I was surprised at what happened one day.

My boss resigned suddenly, although it had been coming for days due to her difficulties in managing a company dedicated to taxes. Almost immediately, the other surprise came: in a short and informal meeting, I was appointed as general president for that nationwide company. At that time, I realized the times of God are exact and wise.

I thought, *I didn't want to sell my small business, and now I am the president of one of the largest tax companies in the United States.* It was unbelievable. I was dancing in the clouds, but at the same time, I thought this was the result of my decisions, work, effort, and sacrifices and somehow was the reward for the planning I'd done a long time ago. Of course, I never had told myself, *I will be the president*, but getting to a position like that is a dream come true for anyone, I believe.

What else could I ask for from life and from God? I thought to myself. *I am the president; I have my life almost resolved; and apart from that, I can do many things for my people.* As some would say, I had heaven in my hands.

My job now was a lot more complicated than I'd thought. I was traveling from one place to another and meeting with all kinds of people, including great executives, national and international politicians, community leaders, businessmen, partners, staff, future members, and more. It was a busy and complicated life. I traveled around the country carrying out the message from the tax company.

Under my hand, we opened more than 162 new offices throughout the country, which are working today for the Latino community. New services were implemented in each of the offices to make life easier for Latinos by providing all of our services in one place. Taxes, notary services, English classes, accounting, and payroll were the service package offered to our clients. We tried to provide any service they needed to avoid their having to go from one place to another in search of what they needed.

Since I was hardly in my locality, it was impossible to be in contact with those who had been my clients in the past, but I had known that was going to happen, because it was part of the deal from the sale of my tax company. The idea was that my business would gradually dissolve as time went by; the name, the photos, and everything the company represented would disappear to become the new business I was representing at that time. However, it seemed my clients missed me, as they kept asking about me.

But my work at that national level absorbed me almost completely. The trips, the creation of new venues, the trainings, and the meetings consumed all my time. It was, without a doubt, a wonderful job and a tremendous opportunity for improvement and growth, from which I would take and learn everything I could. I got a lot of satisfaction during my stay as vice president and then president of that company. I have to highlight the creation of new venues and the collaboration with future entrepreneurs.

Having the opportunity to train a new entrepreneur is something great. Listening to people say, "I do not know if I can, if I am capable, if I have the conditions, or if I have enough money," and then working with them step by step, little by little, and taking them through the whole process, teaching them, showing them they can do it, and letting them see that things are not as complicated as they seem. Goals are not simple, but they can be achieved. Seeing them, after some time, smiling, being happy, and opening and inaugurating their own businesses is priceless. It's something that fills your whole soul and spirit. It fills your whole being with the best and most valuable vibes and energies.

It is wonderful when a person who has been in situations as dark and negative as the ones I lived approaches me to ask for help and advice, and after a few minutes, he or she is telling me his or her personal story. I get to know so much about people that it seems I've known them forever, and they begin to be part of myself. It is as if there is a personal commitment and not just a commercial one. It is wonderful.

You only need to make the decision to be successful and to have the desire to do good things, clear objectives, and huge energy to put into life and into action toward what you want to do. It doesn't matter who you are or what you have been. Your studies, your language, and many other things don't matter. If you have had problems, if you have experience or not, or if you are young or old, man or woman, it doesn't matter if you want to be successful.

To be successful, you only need to have a clear and determined mind, and let yourself be guided by people who have already lived and experienced that process in a successful way. Discovering these truths with others makes me happy, because this means we can all be successful and happy. Unfortunately, few people make the decision to move forward to achieve better things independently. Instead, they prefer to stay where they are, doing what makes them happy, working for others, and helping others to become rich and powerful and not doing it for themselves.

Not everything in my life has been wonderful all the time; I have had many complicated and difficult moments. I don't believe there is a single human being on earth, no matter how successful he or she has been or is, who can say he or she has never had complicated moments, weaknesses, or failures. We all go through difficulties at some point. Some people face immensely more negative conditions than others, but in the end, those situations put us on stony ground on which to walk. I am not an exception to those situations.

In my childhood and adolescence, I had to live submerged in a world full of crimes of all kinds, and although I knew it was negative to be part of those, I was convinced it was normal because everyone who lived there participated directly or indirectly in that world. I told you that part of the past so you would know where I came from and the world I left behind. Today I have nothing to do with that world, those crimes, or that life, but I do have problems of a different nature.

I do have one tie to that life: the huge desire to help people who find themselves in those same muddy and swampy waters or have some kind of problem with drugs or alcohol and need a helping hand, advice, a counselor, a guide, a shoulder to lean on, or someone to listen.

Whatever you propose is possible if you wish and work hard to achieve it. There are no barriers for those who are clear-minded, don't give up, and do not let themselves be overcome by obstacles and controversies.

I have a big commitment with myself. I can't—and I don't want to—hide that my life was difficult as a child and that it was marked by sadness, failures, fears, hunger, poverty, robberies and other crimes, bad moments, and disappointments. I also had some successes, good moments, dreams, and hopes, and above all, I had many plans and desires to move forward every day and achieve many things, no matter where I was or where I wanted to go. I am sure that every time I meet a goal, I will have another one much bigger and more important already planned.

I don't forget where I come from, and for that reason, one of my biggest commitments is to help and encourage people, youngsters especially, to get ahead, not stop, achieve their goals, study, stand out, and not become part of the heap. I want them to seek and work for positive opportunities. I want them to change bad thoughts into positive ones; act in the same way; and, in time, become an example for other children and help those who come after them.

Among the things I try to do is to share with young people and talk to them. I talk to them about the reality of life, the truth. I tell them that television characters and dramatizations are the product of commercial minds looking to sell to and generate audiences. They try little to educate and help, and they are not real but fictional. I ask them to wake up, act, do things for themselves, and not wait for others to do things for them. I encourage them and tell them that young people have to focus on something good, something positive. If they want a car, jewelry, or wealth—whatever they want—they have to work, make positive changes, and do things that last for a lifetime. Drugs and other things can give money, but in the end, they only generate more problems, and that happiness is only temporary, while the problems remain forever and can even lead to death.

I make them understand that they have positive things, a lot of energy, and many skills and qualities waiting to be activated, to pinch them and get them to work for their own welfare and benefit. I make them realize that they have to know themselves, know who they are, be clear about that, and let positive influences change them and mold them. They can listen to negative influences to know them and identify whom they are expressed by, but they must never follow them or pay attention to them, just take them and put them in the trash.

It was always a cause for celebration and joy when someone else managed to open his or her own office. To my fortune and pride, I was the architect of those achievements of many people in the United States.

17

NEW WINDS

The new business was a great school of learning and practice. I learned many things there. I was able to develop a large number of programs and open several offices in many cities around the country—162 total—under my presidency.

The job involved holding meetings to which we invited members of the community interested in opening and running their own business. There we explained the process to become an entrepreneur with us and the conditions they needed to meet. We supported them throughout the process and gave them all the advice and resources necessary for their initiative to succeed and not fail halfway. I made sure to provide complete and excellent customer service and to educate our partners in our philosophy.

I personally participated in many of the training sessions. I met and shook hands with many of the new entrepreneurs, and I am proud to say that somehow, I am part of their success. Many of them were Latinos who were eager to get ahead.

It would be worthwhile to take a short pause in discussing taxes and businesses to talk about other dreams and companies that took my time.

While I was building and working in my company, I was also dedicated to creating new companies in different fields, all of them with clear goals and objectives. Obviously, each one of them was aimed at a particular market after analysis of the market and its growth potential.

It is not a secret that the construction field is in constant development and always in motion. This field is always in need of personnel and companies that can develop projects, provide quality, and guarantee each job. With those and other perspectives in mind, I created a contractor company dedicated to performing construction, getting contracts of different natures, contributing enormously to the economy, and, of course, providing many job opportunities to people year-round. The company always has contracts at the local and state levels, in which we always demonstrate compliance, responsibility, quality, professionalism, and an absolute guarantee on each job completed.

It has been almost eight years since the creation of this company, and throughout all these years, we have always demonstrated clear principles, and we have never failed to meet any of the challenges or complete any of the contracts awarded to us. It is an honor to say that this business is a leader in our market. It is a class-A construction company certified by the Virginia Department of Professional and Occupational Regulation.

Because of the market we are in, we have had the good luck and opportunity to learn about all aspects related to the leasing of commercial and residential properties. We found that the Latino community was lacking a trustworthy company they could rely on and where English speakers could find different alternatives and different services.

Well, there was another business opportunity. I decided to risk a little, and I founded a company that provides leasing of commercial and residential properties. With this company, I have the opportunity to diversify my company portfolio, cover a broader market, ensure quality service, and, of course, try to bring customers from one company to another within my own market.

After more than three years with this company, I have been able to provide excellent services to the community in general and have found it is best to be there when people need a company to trust. Fortunately, my name is well known, and people know and recognize that my name on a project guarantees that it is good.

I feel happy to talk about this topic, because it has been the result of hard work, many experiences, much suffering, dedication, and professionalism. Of course, behind all this, there are many people who have helped me and without whom none of my companies would be what they are today.

Within my own business growth, another idea came to my mind. Riding through the city streets, I realized there were many neglected properties. I thought if those properties were revitalized and fixed up, surely their prices would increase, and of course, the appearance of the areas they were located in would improve. The changes in those properties would mean an increase in their prices, more security, better schools and roads, and general development and improvement for the communities around them.

Without hesitation, I sat down, started writing, and founded my next company, dedicated to property investment. The commercial goal of this company is basically to buy, repair, and then sell properties.

It is a wonderful business, but it's not as easy or simple as it seems, because the real estate business is risky. Today you might have good prices, but from one moment to another, the prices might drop, and all your profits might become losses.

This last company has been in the market for almost six years, and since its inception, it has had impressive results. Every day it grows more and more, and every day more people are looking for us to be that link between their investment and the property they are looking to buy or want to sell.

I cannot say that all these ideas have been with me from the beginning. No, not at all. They are a product of the learning acquired as time passes.

As I have said, goals and objectives are adjusted as time passes and as needed, and when things don't come out as planned, it is necessary to stop, observe, analyze, and adjust if necessary. I have done something like that each time I needed to or considered it appropriate.

In the world, there is an almost unlimited amount of opportunities and ideas waiting to be developed and exploited. Sometimes people do not even realize them, and they go through life without stopping to see and think about what surrounds them, what they have, what there is, and what there is not. They are like sleepwalkers wandering around the world, and they only dedicate themselves to the routine of their lives day to day. They're like human machines in that everything they do, they do it mechanically, out of habit. Such a person is like a marionette: it only does what it was designed for and will never be able to do something by itself; it is predetermined and predisposed to do only that for which it was designed. In the same way, many people go around the world, and they do not change, progress, or evolve. They are like marionettes, waiting for someone to move their parts to do or feel something. Many of us have seen zombie movies. These people are something like that: dead in life. They got used to doing nothing more than what is customary and what they were asked to or had to do to receive a minimum amount of money and pay bills every month.

I recognize that starting is difficult and frightening, and we hesitate all the time because we do not want to fail. All of this is reasonable, but if you don't start, if you don't dare, how will you know what you can achieve? How will you know how far you can go? You have to take risks and try; it's the only way to know and be sure.

If things do not go as you intended, yes, that's bad, but it's not the end. Even the greatest inventors in the world, in technology and other fields, tried many times before being successful with their ideas. So if you're not successful on the first try, try again. Apply the experiences and lessons from that first time to the second time. Always remember to take the good from the bad and the best from the good. Each experience, no matter how bad it is, always leaves you a lesson. Take advantage of those lessons! Make them useful.

You can't give up. Giving up is the answer of cowards, the mediocre, and the lazy. I know because I experienced it. At some point, you will feel like giving up, but don't worry; that is temporary. When you reinitiate your plans and apply all your heart and the lessons learned from that first time, you'll see that each time, things get simpler, the processes are easier, and the results are bigger and better.

As you achieve your goals, you will see that new ideas, projects, and opportunities come to you. Analyze them, think calmly, and share them with the people you trust. Ask them for their opinions, and make the decision you think is the best one for you, your plans, and your future.

I am telling you this with experience and knowledge: the more you climb, the more difficult things will turn, because you will always want to be more successful, make things better, avoid making mistakes, and be almost perfect. Those things wear one down a lot.

I don't mean to imply that you will become another person, a different human being, from the person you were when you started to be successful. No, not at all. As you go up, you have the obligation to be humbler. Don't forget that the higher you get, your success doesn't mean you are more than others. The greatness of human beings is measured when they are at the top, at their highest point, not when they are down or when they fall. Also, remember, the more you go up, the harder the fall, and as you fall, you will see on the way down those people you helped or humiliated at some stage of your life, so keep your humility and simplicity, and don't stop being human and fair.

Nowadays, I have several kinds of companies, but I still have a long way to go, and I can still improve. For some individuals, I will seem too ambitious or too concerned about money, but at some point in life, you realize there are still many opportunities to exploit, and if there are no people with the initiative, you can be the one to take that initiative and explore new horizons. In addition, situations change overnight and force you to rethink your plans and restart new challenges.

After almost a year and a half as president of a big company, having developed a wonderful career, opened a large number of offices nationwide, trained a large number of new business owners, made hundreds of presentations, and participated in countless meetings at both the national and international level, my time at that company came to an end.

The truth is that the big owner of those tax companies, which are considered the largest nationwide, got into some businesses that led him to complicated matters, which caused him to be fired by the general manager of the company, even though he had the majority of the shares. It was a commercial move that altered a great business infrastructure as well as many companies and many people's lives. One of those people was me.

When I'd agreed to sell my business and accept the position of vice president, I'd made a contract with the general owner of those businesses in which I would keep a percentage of the work I did, plus other benefits. Unfortunately, he wanted to retract what we'd agreed upon and approached me with some proposals that had nothing to do with what we had agreed to in the beginning. That obviously generated huge disappointment for me, as I personally had invested a lot in the company because I really believed in the results and its philosophy.

With that situation, everything I believed in was going down the sewer. Everything I had done for the company was worth it because I helped many people to be successful, but on a personal level, it didn't provide me with what I considered fair. My compensation, work hours, travel, training, and own time, part of my personal life, were there in that national company, that monster that now didn't fit me in the same way I had fit it and assumed my commitment to it.

That was something I could not accept. I had already lost some money with them, which I accepted because I knew that the other part of my earnings was bigger and more important, because I didn't want to pay more attention to it. But when I got the news that I would not receive what had been agreed upon, I had to make harder decisions and leave the company almost immediately.

I was forced to hire a lawyer to take care of my case and try to recover what legally belonged to me. Now the matter is in the courts, waiting for a judge to hear the case and render a verdict. I am convinced I will get what I earned with my work.

This is another lesson I want you to learn: it doesn't matter whom you do business with, including how famous, rich, poor, or known the other person is; always make sure you have clear contracts in which you specify each detail and question, and discuss the small print in the contracts. If you do not understand, do not sign. Find out and investigate, but do not sign. If you are being pressured to sign without giving yourself the opportunity to ask, it is because something strange is behind whatever is being offered to you.

That was the end of a cycle that I thought was beneficial in my life. The great company with tentacles at the national level vanished like water and sand in my hands. However, on the other hand, I was sure that everything was better and that if it was God's time for me to leave that company under those circumstances, that was my decision as well.

Soon after, everything was much clearer. In a meeting with a colleague in California, I discovered that the exit from that company was the beginning of a giant project I have begun to develop with the woman who is now my wife. With the emotional support of our two little ones, we have begun to work together to start a new family business to assist the community around us.

18

A NEW PATH

Many people still have the image of first business in their minds and memory for a reason.

While I was in charge and managing this company, everything was done the right way, with honesty, compliance, and the highest standards of quality. I was always available to all my clients and always approached them with the same warmth, cordialness, and professionalism. Obviously, that generates a wonderful reputation and image.

Both the reputation and the image of that company remain intact in the memories and perceptions of the community members, who keep asking for me and following me wherever I go, so I can provide them with my professional services.

I have always believed that people deserve to be treated well and to receive excellent services and all the respect in the world. My wife and I decided to create a new company like the previous one but improved and revitalized. We put all our past experiences and lessons into practice within our new company.

It was not easy to restart due to my sudden exit from the business where I'd worked for a while. I had already created a long-term work plan there because I'd been convinced that company had great potential. In addition, there were many things that could have been done for the community. Anyway, that issue is over, and I don't want to go deeper into that.

There were several difficulties I had to overcome before putting myself into the business world again. I had to solve some legal issues that somehow tied me to the previous company but in no way would be an impediment to continue growing and making my new dream come true with my wife and the mother of my two little girls.

After consulting with some lawyers and considering different options, we made the decision to create this company. A great businessman from California helped me with the name. He has several tax companies there that have almost the same brand, and their success has been resounding.

Hands-on, we initiated all the necessary steps to open the type of company we wanted. We applied for the necessary permits and licenses to carry out the tasks and functions we now offer to the entire community. We started hiring qualified staff to occupy each of the positions we had open. We trained our staff not only to know the economic reason for what we do but also to know, practice, and share our business philosophy.

Of course, in order to start our business, we made a detailed market analysis in order to know the ideal place to set up our company. That was not a simple thing, because the success of a company greatly depends on that study. Not knowing where to set up a business or choosing the wrong place can doom a business from the start.

We took all the necessary steps to ensure our new business was assured of success from the beginning. Of course, you can't always guarantee the future of a company, but at least when you know you have anticipated everything, it is more likely your business will have a promising future.

My new company was born from the prevailing need in the community for a brand in which customers could trust without restrictions and find not only the necessary services but also the confidence of being backed up by a reliable and known name with a high level of responsibility, knowledge, and honesty.

I had the blessing of walking that road hand in hand with my wife and my angels. They are the pillars not only of this company and those to come in the future but also of my own life. Thanks to them, today I have a clear and defined idea of what I wish my life to be from now on. Without a doubt, the three of them, and the children who will come down the road when God decides, are my life.

I am not exaggerating when I say what I think and feel for my family. My wife came into my life at a special and definitive moment, and she gave me the light I needed to get out of where I was. Above all, she taught me the importance of recognizing our mistakes, being honest with ourselves, and knowing that it's never too late to go back, ask for forgiveness if needed, and adjust all the screws of the gears so that the machinery continues to work as good as new or even better than before.

Sweetie, you are the lighthouse in the distance that guides my steps and brings me to the mainland when I am wrecking in the sea of doubts and uncertainties. Our new company actually is your business creation and your baby in the business world.

This business was born not only to be a company that provides services—tax preparation; notaries; translations; taxes for homes, cars, and businesses; payroll; establishment of business licenses; and more—but also to grow and develop as a leading company. It has already opened its second branch in the metro area.

We knew in advance that once the community found out we had opened this business, they wouldn't hesitate to request our services and become our clients.

In this world, as a result of experience, one finds people who have good ideas and initiatives who only need a little push of help and support to get ahead. In addition, they demonstrate with their attitude and work the desire to do big and important things. The new branch is the product of the initiative of a great character who, for some time, was looking for an opportunity to develop the seed he had inside. He is a restless man who decided to put his mind to his goal and is now receiving the fruits of his labors.

He already had a lot of experience as a businessman, but due to different circumstances, he had temporarily withdrawn from the business world, and he was again in search of a great opportunity to develop what he wanted. Once again, it doesn't matter who you are or the experience you have or don't have; if you want it, look for it, and work hard, you get it. This is for certain.

We have returned to the local commercial world, we are in full swing and growth, and nothing is going to stop us. We are going ahead with everything, and we have a service for everyone. This new entrepreneurial effort was born to stay and to solidify itself as the first company engaged in Latin services in the entire metropolitan area.

I wanted to leave for the end of this chapter a topic that makes me proud, not only for what it represents for me professionally and personally but also because from my own standpoint, I think it is a point of pride for the Latino community I represent in some ways.

In October 2017, I was invited as an expert on the US Hispanic market by the Integra Institute and the National Commission of Mexico for the Protection and Defense of Financial Services Users (CONDUSEF) to the second round-table discussion with the president of CONDUSEF, senior executives of Mexican and US financial institutions, executives of money-transfer companies, and Mexican and US government officials, which took place on October 26, 2017, in Mexico City.

The Integra Institute is comprised of entrepreneurs, students, and professionals. Its mission is to contribute to the professional and intellectual development of the Mexican community residing in the United States. CONDUSEF is a government agency that promotes and provides education and financial transparency so users are informed of the decisions they make about benefits, costs, and risks offered by the Mexican financial system, as well as how to protect their interests by supervising and regulating financial institutions.

The topics discussed were many and important, including

- the opportunities and challenges of the financial inclusion of Mexicans living in the United States and Mexico;
- the area of opportunity of the remittance market between Mexico and the United States;
- how to give financial power to Mexicans living in the United States; and
- how to collectively finance technology that can benefit Mexicans who live in the United States and their families in Mexico.

I had the opportunity to participate in the round-table discussion and provide my points of view and experiences from my work with the Latino community on a national level.

The new administration of the United States has made changes to the tax system, and that issue was included in the discussions, to learn a little more about its repercussions for taxpayers, especially for the Mexican and Latino community who reside in the United States.

The event was a great experience and a great opportunity to exchange ideas, share other perspectives, contribute my knowledge to all the attendees, and, of course, make new contacts who represent opportunities of all kinds.

19

WHAT IF?

Many times, I have wondered what would have happened to my life if I had been born into a normal family. When I say *normal*, I mean a father who lives and stays at home; a mother who does not suffer from the situations my mother lived; and, above all, the presence of someone to guide me, advise me, and help me in the key moments and difficult situations that all human beings go through.

I imagine that if I had been born into that normal family, I would not have delivered marijuana, been a car thief, gotten into trouble with firearms, or gone to prison. Maybe I would have gone to school, received a scholarship for sports, and ended up in a university. Most likely, I would have been a professional in a sport, and at this age, I would be retired and would be a coach at a school or university.

Another option is that I would have become one of those kids whose parents gave them everything. I would have graduated from university, had my own car, dressed in brand-name clothes, and had everything because my boss—my father—overprotected me and gave me everything.

I am certain I would not have had to suffer all the negative familial, social, and economic experiences my situation forced upon me and many other young people in life.

But no, I was born into a somewhat different family. My dad was almost never at home, and my mother suffered from different situations. My two older sisters did their best to help, but it was not enough. I grew up without authority or order. My parents just talked to me to scold me and shout at me. So my life, my world, was outside, where I found what I didn't have at home and where people told me what I wanted to hear. Well, today I think that was their game: to make others happy so those individuals would do what they wanted them to do for them.

As I said, I was convinced I would not make it to eighteen years old. The environment I was in and the things I did led me to that thought. In addition, many young people did not reach eighteen in our community. My best friend died at sixteen, and I always wondered, *Will I be next? Will I wake up alive tomorrow? What about next week?*

I wonder, if I had not lived those negative experiences, would there have been a time when I would have asked myself, "What are you doing with your life?" Or when my grandfather told me, "You're wasting your life. Do something positive with it"? Certainly not, because I would have had a mediocre half life. Maybe it would have been a successful life for many, because I would have had a job that gave me enough money to pay the bills, but I would not have had half of what I have today and what I'm projecting to have and would not have lived the amount of experiences both positive and negative in my life. Nor would I be the person I consider myself to be, with my human qualities and, of course, defects, as any human being has.

I am aware that many of those experiences are not to be proud of, but that was my life. I lived it and enjoyed it while it lasted, just as I live and enjoy my life today. All those experiences gave me the wisdom and creative ideas to get ahead and not give up. They shielded me against all storms, including the evil, betrayals, and envy of some people who have come into my life. All that is a product of the bad and negative situations of my life.

I repeat: those are not things to be proud of or to fan out about as peacocks do, but it was my life. It was what I had to live, and I lived it for my own good and the good of those who were at my side. The advantage was that I got ahead, reconsidered, restructured my path, and straightened out what was crooked.

It doesn't matter where you come from or what you have done; if you want a positive change in your life, there is always a way to go.

There are always opportunities presented to us. We just have to take them, like when someone throws us a life ring in the middle of the sea. We have to hold on to it because it will keep us afloat. But everything depends on you and no one else.

If you want to be successful and leave the dark tunnel you are in or just take a step forward, do it right now. Don't stop; don't let your wings be cut off. The moment is now. Don't leave for tomorrow what you can do right now, because tomorrow there will be someone occupying the position and the opportunity you wasted today, and that opportunity will be gone.

When I say *right now*, I do not mean to go out in a hurry to do things. What I'm trying to say is that now is the time, the precise moment, to start planning what you want to be and do in your future. If an idea or a project comes into your head that you wish to develop, put it into action. Don't keep it inside your mind, because it won't bloom there. It's as if you have a plant with the most beautiful of flowers, but if you do not water it, take care of it, and take it out in the sun, that flower will die and will never give more beautiful flowers. It will dry up, and from it, only a memory will remain.

You have to do the same thing with what you want to accomplish in your life. You have to develop a plan and adjust things that you don't think are good for you and your project. Talk with other people who have experience in that environment and who can help you, and search the internet for resources that exist in the community where you live. See if your local, state, or federal government offers help and resources for people like you. Talk to your pastor or priest if you are a believer. Participate in training classes related to your project. Remember that in many places, you can find people who can give you ideas without having to specifically talk about your project. Search and ask, but do not stand still. Move.

You have to be clear in your mind that you can achieve, are capable, and can and will be successful. Don't take your mind off that. Remove bad things—negative thoughts, bad friendships, bad advice and counselors. Eradicate the negative vibes from your being and your environment. Those negative vibes affect not only your project or company but also you and the people around you.

Don't stay with the memory; take a chance right now, and take the bull by the horns. Nothing in life is big enough that you can't achieve it; you just have to make the decision to do it.

Unfortunately, there is no one who can do it for you. There are others who will develop the idea for you, show it to the world, create jobs and opportunities, and make your idea a resounding success, but of course, they will keep it, and you will be sorry for not having been more daring and risky. You will be watching as your idea moves everywhere while you continue meditating, thinking, and seeing the triumph of others with what you had in mind.

Remember, it doesn't matter who you are, where you come from, the language you speak, the color of your skin, what you have made of your life in the past, or the joys or sufferings of your life. None of that matters if you are clear on what you want to achieve. Of course, all the ingredients I just mentioned are going to be part of your recipe, but they are not the real reason to develop your idea and project.

I repeat: those are just experiences. Experiences can be used to your benefit but can't limit or minimize the chances of success. On the contrary, those are the ingredients of the recipe for success that will give a better taste, color, texture, and smell to the project you want to start.

Remember that everything takes sacrifice and work and involves an effort. Not everything comes for free; by inheritance; or because you are tall, pretty, blond, black, Latin, Asian, or anything else. Opportunities are not like that. We have to plan, work, analyze, and do. We cannot remain static; we always have to be moving and looking for solutions, ideas, improvements, changes, and new services or projects.

Those who stay pinned at their desks will die in the next season. Those who don't change or get up to date are destined to be static and buried in oblivion and the abandonment of their clients.

To survive, sustain, and continue in the market, you are obliged to change; modify; and inject new blood, new energy, promotions, discounts, marketing, and a range of strategies that will help make your business, your name, and your brand grow every day and not disappear.

I would like to give an example of the importance of these words. Earlier, I talked about a great man who helped me many years ago when I worked with Jackson Hewitt. He gave me the opportunity to start in his company, learn how to prepare taxes, and put into practice my knowledge of accounting. He had twenty-three tax-service offices and appointed me manager of an office for the first time in my life. Unfortunately, he didn't put into practice strategies and suggestions for changes, updates, and training and failed in a resounding way. Today he doesn't have one office left out of the twenty-three. The emporium he created with work and sacrifice stayed in the past. He didn't make changes, he didn't make updates to the technology, and advances took their toll. As a result, he ended up losing everything he'd built over the years.

Keep updating, training, changing, and bringing new ideas to your business and projects so they stay current, vibrant, eye-catching, and popular.

20

TO THE COMMUNITY

I believe that what we achieve and obtain in life is a product not of chance but of a series of steps and situations we realize little by little as time passes.

Of course, the people who surround us are a fundamental part of the process, and I mean everyone, from customers to our workers, the government workers who approve licenses and permits and check information, suppliers, and our families.

As active members of the community, we have an obligation—not a legal one but a moral and internal one—to help and to give what we receive, returning some of the help and support that other members of the community give us. It's not a secret that without our clients, we would not exist, and we would not have reached the places we have reached. What better way to reward them than by helping and participating in social, cultural, and sporting events and celebrations?

Keep in mind that it is not only financial aid that is important and necessary but also another kind of help. Be present, be supportive, and say, "I am with you." Express opinions and use words that help and motivate others to get ahead.

In my life, I have had and still have the wonderful opportunity to share my story and my experiences with children and young people.

I didn't want people to know what I was as a youngster; I would have preferred to hide that, take it with me to the grave, and leave it there forever. I thought that way for years. However, time and positive influences made me change my opinion.

I take no pride in saying that I was a criminal and was in jail; that is not an example for anyone. However, that was part of my life. Other people have their secrets and things that are not so pretty to tell and share about their lives.

After traveling many paths, meeting many people, learning their stories, and reading many others, in addition to the lessons, wisdom, and maturity that, fortunately, the years gave me, I understand that the past is past and that what I am today is from today and is part of my future. I also understand that what I experienced, although it is not nice to tell, can help many to understand and accept their realities and, even better, to understand and reconsider that there are positive possibilities and that they can be successful and succeed in life in spite of the things that have marked their past. It is not easy—I know that—but it is not as difficult as it seems. It is far from impossible.

With all this in mind, I decided to open my heart, soul, and head to tell people, including my community and my son, the truth about my life. Few would suspect that the person they see in the streets was in jail at the age of eighteen and distributed marijuana when he was just an elementary school student.

Perhaps the most important thing for me, and what I want to invest most of my time and effort in, is talking with young people and children. I want to make them understand that life is not easy, the world unfolds in a crazy way, there are people of all kinds around them, and it is important to know who they are and whom they have by their side as friends or partners. The potential success they may have will depend to a large extent on this.

But also, I would like to tell my story and emphasize that in life, there are opportunities waiting for someone to say, "Here I am! I will be the one to develop that opportunity, make it mature, and let it grow in the community."

I would like young people and children to realize that not everything is the way it seems on television. Not everything is violence, partying, or being on the streets. Drugs and vices do not lead anywhere good. They take us to the hospital, to jail, or to death.

That's the truth and the reality. Sooner or later, those who are involved in drugs and vices will know one or more of the three described above: a hospital, a prison, or death. That is indisputable. Like it or not, it is what it is.

I would like to share that message with them. I am sure many others have told them before, but how many of those people have lived in the world and the life I have? I'm sure none or very few. Believe me, my message is different from the message expressed by those people. We are polar opposites in experience but united by the objective and the message.

In the end, it's much more valuable when someone who has been immersed in these intricate labyrinths of the underworld emerges to tell his experiences; express why it's not good to be there; advise others; and give them good vibes to succeed, be successful, and be beneficial to the community.

For me, it is much more valuable to be able to talk to these people than to have the opportunity to make a donation, sponsor a soccer team, or hold an event. It gives me greater satisfaction to be in direct contact with young people—to see their faces, answer their questions, and address their concerns.

I love doing it, and I will never get tired of it. I will be here when someone wants to invite me to talk. I like to share not only my knowledge and skills but also my life experiences with anyone who approaches me in search of advice and help.

As I said, I sponsor teams and soccer leagues. I love soccer, and every time life allows me, I will do my best to help young people and children who are practicing this sport. I also have been a coach in churches where activities have been developed for the children's welfare.

I collaborate with nonprofit organizations so they can continue carrying out their functions to help the community, and I also provide support to various community events for the cultural and emotional development of the families of immigrants who urgently need our help. It's important that the people who receive this support are really those we want to reach and not others who might not need help or can obtain it through the government or formal institutions.

My support is and will remain focused on the ones who need help the most and, of course, the Latino community and immigrants in general.

My business participating and assisting in El Juguetazo, a cultural celebration among Latinos and Asians in Chesterfield County, Virginia. All children, regardless of language, nationality, or status, receive new and unwrapped gifts in an event full of happiness, joy, fun, and a sense of community.

El Juguetazo event in 2018

My newest business venture
Together with the ambassadors and associates
of AmeraTex and Business Services
A Text Preparation Franchise
August 2020

21

THE GROWTH NEVER STOPS

When I drive through the streets of Virginia, I notice almost everything. I pay attention to advertisements, traffic signs, stores, and people. I pay attention to everything—not gossip or anything like that, but I have learned that you can always find ideas everywhere and in everything. Also, I don't like to go around like a puppet or a doll; I enjoy the scenery and the landscapes on the roads.

This is how my life goes. I pay attention to many things at the same time because I know that at any moment, I can discover an opportunity to continue growing and developing as a merchant and as a professional.

Even the most seemingly stupid and insignificant things can bring great benefits if you have the ability to see and analyze the possibilities of development and growth that may exist—for example, an old shack in a remote corner, a vacant lot near a dumpster, scrap left in some remote place, or a small community of people lacking in services and care.

I could list many more examples, but I think these are enough to make you understand and bring into perspective the idea of always being attentive to opportunities and options to undertake new commercial ventures or to develop the first one. We have to be attentive to the signals that often go unnoticed under our noses without our being aware of them.

I live to hunt those possibilities. I remain attentive to everything I see and anything I believe might have a future in my development. Obviously, there are many things that do not interest me, even if I see potential, because I am not going to and do not want to get into all kinds of businesses. Even if it's something that might be successful in the future, if it is not something I like to do, then I simply leave it so other people who like it can develop it and work in those fields to exploit them and grow within that particular market.

Now, if that opportunity is something that catches my attention and is within my market and interests, then I go hunting, I catch the prey, and I don't let go until I know it is mine and I can move forward.

I am sure I will be working like this in the years to come, starting new companies and giving people the opportunity for a business and personal growth. Not everything I do is for me or for my family. I feel I have a commitment to the community; to young people; and to people who want to get ahead, start their own companies, and be their own bosses.

Those who want to get on this train of success and triumph with me are more than welcome. The doors are open for all as long as they arrive with positivity, energy, and the intent to rise to the occasion and progress. I don't want anyone who comes with the idea of interrupting the triumphant flow of those who wish to progress.

I could not specify at this time the opportunities I would like to explore in the future, but I am aware and open, with fully charged batteries, to detect any opportunity. In addition, I have my office open for those who want to come with their own ideas and need help, support, and professional advice that I and the people who work at my company are willing to provide.

My family life will continue growing and improving. Now I am married, and my wife and I have two beautiful daughters. Together we have a wonderful home. For now, we have no plans to have more children, but you never know. God will tell us or surprise us one day with that happy news.

Without hesitation, I will continue to make every effort to talk with young people and children about the negative issues that surround the youth of today. More importantly, I can also tell them about the positive things life offers and the ways in which every one of us can be part of and take advantage of those nice and good things life has for all of us, no matter who we are.

Growth and development cannot be stopped. You can do whatever you want, no matter where or with whom. There will always come a time when the environment forces you to change, evolve, and improve, and if you don't do it, shame on you. These words, although they seem like a tongue-twister, are true: we must change as the change changes so that the change does not change us.

Don't stop. Just take a break, breathe hard, and then continue on your way. There is always someone behind you wanting to outdo you and leave you lying in the road. It is your responsibility to always be awake and attentive. Progress, dare, advance, and grow, but don't forget that you are a human being and that you are surrounded by other human beings who need you and who can also give you a hand at some point in your life.

It does not matter who you are or what you have been. It matters what you want and plan to be.

Remember to surround yourself with good people. Keep your family together, and always keep God in your thoughts. It doesn't matter if the situation is negative; God never abandons you. He will always be with you and will carry you in his arms when the road becomes narrow and steep. Keep God in your heart and in your whole being.

Printed in the United States
By Bookmasters